A TESTAMENT OF JOY

LUMINAIRE STUDIES

A TESTAMENT OF
JOY

Studies in Philippians

DAVID EWERT

WINNIPEG, MB CANADA   KINDRED PRODUCTIONS   HILLSBORO, KS USA

Published simultaneously by Kindred Productions, Winnipeg Manitoba R2L 2E5 and Kindred Productions, Hillsboro, Kansas 67063

Cover design by Lee Toews, TS Design Associates, Winnipeg
Book design by Fred Koop, Winnipeg
Printed in Canada by The Christian Press, Winnipeg

Canadian Cataloguing in Publication Data
Ewert, David, 1922-

A testament of joy
(Luminaire studies)
"The English version ... is that of the New Revised Standard Version."
Includes bibliographical references.
ISBN 0-921788-21-5

1. Bible . N.T. Philippians - Commentaries.
I. Title. II Series.

BS2705.3.E94 1995 227', 6077 C95-920029-0

International Standard Book Number: 0-921788-21-5

TABLE OF CONTENTS

Preface

By adding another volume to the *Luminaire* series of commentaries, one hopes Bible study groups will be encouraged in their efforts to understand the message of the biblical writers and translate that message into everyday life.

Paul's letter to the Philippians has always been a favorite among Bible readers and it is my prayer the study of this epistle will bring the readers some of that joy which the apostle experienced when he wrote it long ago.

Philippians is a "prison epistle" written by the apostle Paul who, in the words of Peter, was "moved by the Holy Spirit" (2 Peter 1:21). Although he is long dead, Paul continues to speak to the church today through his "open" letters.

What makes Philippians so unique is its joyful tone. This is hardly what one expects from a man who has been robbed of his freedom not because he committed some crime, but because he had spread the good news of the gospel. This letter demonstrates how the Christian faith can triumph even in the midst of tragedy and suffering. It is in fact a "Testament of Joy."

Joy is a recurring theme in the writings of Paul, in spite of the fact so much of his life was marked by pain and suffering. The words which Paul uses for joy in this letter have a secular background and originally described a mood dependent on physical comfort, well-being or health. Paul, however, uses them with a new meaning in the context of the believer's experience of the saving grace of God proclaimed in the gospel. The apostle has "baptized" the words joy and rejoice into Christ and so Christian joy is no longer dependent on health, wealth, comfort or general well-being. Christian joy is ultimately rooted in an unshakable faith in God and springs from the deep conviction the believer's life is in the hands of a loving heavenly Father. Joy is the hallmark of the new age that dawned with Christ's coming. In the words of Paul to the Romans "The kingdom of God is not food and drink, but ...joy in the Holy Spirit"(14:17). Joy embraces both elation and depression, delight and dismay, all the ups and downs of life. And so we have chosen as a title for this study of Philippians "A Testament of Joy."

As in other *Luminaire* volumes this commentary is divided into thirteen chapters and can be covered in one quarter of the church year. At the end of each chapter the reader will find review questions designed to draw out some of the practical implications of the text for everyday life in the twentieth century.

Although the commentary is based on the Greek text, I have tried to write in non-technical language. The English version quoted as a rule throughout the commentary is the New Revised Standard Version

David Ewert

CHAPTER ONE

Introduction to the Letter

Of the twenty-one letters found in the New Testament, thirteen are attributed to the apostle Paul. Interestingly, at least five of these Pauline epistles were written from prison. Normally, Ephesians, Colossians, Philippians and Philemon are classified as Prison Epistles. (2 Timothy, which was also written from prison, belongs to the Pastoral Epistles.) Philippians stands somewhat apart from the other three Prison Epistles in that it was addressed to a church in Macedonia; the other three were carried by Tychicus to readers who lived in the province of Asia. It was certainly not the last time that letters from prison turned out to be a source of great inspiration to their readers. Our century, too, has witnessed the publication of profoundly moving letters from prison, even though such modern writers cannot claim divine inspiration or apostolic authority, as does the apostle Paul. Before us, then, lies a letter, written by a man who suffered incredible hardships for the sake of his Christian witness, but who refused to let the tragedies of this life quench that holy joy which pervades this epistle. We begin our study of this choice piece of Christian writing with some comments on the city of Philippi, in which the readers lived.

I. THE CITY OF PHILIPPI

On his second missionary journey Paul, Silas and Timothy came
to the city of Troas, under the guidance of the Spirit of Jesus. In this
coastal city Paul had a vision of a man from Macedonia who begged
him to come over to Macedonia and help people there (Acts 16:9).
Paul and his colleagues understood this as a summons from God and
so they sailed for Neapolis, the port about thirteen kilometers from
the city of Philippi. Luke speaks of Philippi as "the leading city of
Macedonia and a Roman colony " (Acts 16:12).

The city of Philippi derives its name from Philip 11 of Macedon,
who founded it in 356 B.C. Philip, the father of Alexander the Great,
was particularly interested in the gold and silver mines nearby. Also,
the city commanded the land route to the Hellespont and Asia.
Philippi remained insignificant until the Roman conquest of Macedonia in 168-167 B.C. In 42 B.C. Philippi became the scene of the battle between the forces of Mark Antony and Octavian and those of
Brutus and Cassius, the assassins of Julius Caesar. Brutus and Cassius were defeated. After the battle of Actium (31 B.C.) at which Octavian (emperor Augustus) emerged triumphant, Philippi, which had
by now become a Roman colony, was enlarged and a good number
of veteran Roman soldiers settled here. The city then got the rather
honorific name: Colonia Iulia Augusta Philippensis.

As a Roman colony, the constitution of Philippi was modeled on
that of the mother city Rome. The citizens of a Roman colony were
seen as Roman citizens. Like most Roman colonies, Philippi had two
chief magistrates (called *strategoi*. Acts 16:22,35,36,38). These magistrates were attended by lictors bearing bundles of rods as badges of
their office (Luke calls them "rod-bearers," Acts 16:35,38). There may
be an allusion to the privileged position of the Philippians as Roman
citizens in Philippians 1:27 and 3:20.

Philippi was situated in Macedonia. By the fourth century B.C.
Philip 11, of Macedonia had made himself master of the city-states of
Greece. Alexander the Great, his son, inherited this Greco-Macedon-
ian domain and made it the base for his conquest of Asia (up to the
Indus Valley) and Egypt. However, after his death when his empire
was divided, Macedonia became a separate kingdom once more. On

a pretext the Romans declared war on Macedonia in 197 B.C. and again in 168 B.C.. Finally, Macedonia became a Roman province with four geographical districts. The Romans then built a military road, the Egnatian Way, across the province, connecting Dyrrachium on the Adriatic with Philippi and its port, Neapolis (modern Kavalla), and later still to Byzantium on the Bosporus. In Paul's day the proconsul (the governor of a senatorial province) of Macedonia had his seat of administration at Thessalonica.

II. THE CHURCH AT PHILIPPI

After the middle of the first century Paul and his companions (Luke was now with the missionary team) arrived in Philippi. Paul's usual practice when visiting a Gentile city was to seek out a Jewish synagogue, where he was usually assured of an audience of Jews and God-fearing Gentiles who had been attracted to the synagogue. Although only ten adult males were required to form a regular Jewish congregation, Philippi, so it seems, did not have such a synagogue. But there was an informal meeting place outside the city by the river where some women gathered for prayers on the Sabbath day. Among them was a business woman Lydia, a native of Thyatira in Asia Minor, who traded in purple dye. She was most likely a God-fearing woman. As Paul explained the gospel to these women, the Lord opened Lydia's heart and she responded to the message of the apostle (Acts 16:14). Together with her household (which probably included slaves and other dependents) she was baptized and then extended hospitality to Paul and his associates.

However, when Paul exorcised an evil spirit (literally, "a pythonic spirit," suggesting she was thought to be the mouthpiece of the god Apollo) from a slave girl, he got himself and his associates into deep trouble. The masters of the girl, who made their livelihood through the fortune-telling activity of this girl, were deeply annoyed when the source of their income suddenly dried up. Consequently Paul and Silas, the two Jews in the missionary quartet, were dragged before the magistrates in the forum and charged with causing trouble in the city and teaching customs contrary to Roman law (Acts 16:20,21). Bystanders joined in the attack and the magistrates decided to make an example of these unwelcome disturbers of the peace and ordered the lictors to beat them and lock them up in prison. The prison warden made sure they would not escape by fastening their feet in stocks.

When the authorities arrived at the jail next morning, intending to expel the prisoners from Philippi, they faced an embarrassing situation. To their chagrin they discovered Paul and Silas were Roman citizens who had been beaten and imprisoned without a hearing—contrary to Roman justice. The magistrates then apologized for their mistake and earnestly begged the missionaries to leave town. By reminding the authorities of their Roman citizenship, the apostles wanted to assure the new converts of a measure of legal protection. Before leaving town the apostles went to Lydia's house to encourage the new converts.

Luke tells the fascinating story of what happened during the night in which Paul and Silas were incarcerated. An earthquake struck at midnight while Paul and Silas were praying and singing hymns to God. The cell door was broken open and their chains fell off. The jailor was so alarmed when he saw the prisoners were free that he attempted suicide. However, he was marvelously saved when Paul explained to him the message of the gospel (Acts 16:25-34). The jailor and his household were then baptized and he demonstrated his new faith by showing kindness to the missionaries and rejoicing with his entire household. Luke says nothing about the receipt of the Spirit by these new converts, but since joy is a fruit of the Spirit, we have clear evidence of the gift of the Spirit.

How many more converts were added to the church before Paul left Philippi is not known, but clearly he left a young congregation of believers behind as he and his companions made their way to Thessalonica. Paul retained strong links with the Philippian church in the following years. The church in turn regarded Paul with great affection, as can be seen from the fact that they sent gifts to him from time to time (see Phil. 4:15,16).

About five years later he visited the Philippian church, sending Timothy and Erastus to prepare the way for his visit (Acts 19:22). Also, after spending three months in Greece (Acts 20:1,2), he visited Philippi again when he was on his way to Jerusalem with the collection for the saints in Jerusalem. Paul boasts of the generosity of the Macedonian churches, which included Philippi, in his second letter to the Corinthians (2 Cor. 8:15).

III. THE LETTER TO THE PHILIPPIANS

A. The Occasion.

It would appear from Philippians 2:25 that the readers of this letter had sent one of their members, Epaphroditus, for the special purpose of ministering to Paul's needs as the apostle languished in prison. While helping Paul (or perhaps even on his way there) Epaphroditus had become seriously ill—an illness that nearly proved fatal (2:27). This messenger of the Philippian church had brought a gift to alleviate Paul's needs (4:18). Epaphroditus was now ready to return to Philippi and Paul used the occasion to write this friendly letter. In one sense we might think of the letter to the Philippians as a thank-you note.

However, as always when Paul wrote to the churches he had founded, there were other reasons why he wrote to them. Not only did the departure of Epaphroditus provide Paul with an occasion to send along a letter to express his gratitude for their generosity, but it also gave him an opportunity to explain what had happened to Epaphroditus. Lest they should think this messenger of the church had not lived up to his obligations, Paul assures them he risked his life for the sake of the work of Christ (2:25-30).

No doubt the Philippians had also been deeply concerned about Paul's situation, knowing he was in prison awaiting trial. In his letter he reports on his own situation. Moreover, he wants them to know that he will visit them just as soon as he is released, if that should happen (2:24). And just as soon as his own situation has been clarified, he plans to send Timothy to them (2:23).

Over and above these practical reasons for writing to the Philippians, Paul uses the occasion to express his pastoral concerns for them. These can be discussed more conveniently under the next caption.

B. The Purpose.

The purpose of the letter can be inferred from a consideration of its contents. Although the letter is friendly in tone and affectionate in spirit, Paul expresses his concerns about his readers as well. He knows this infant church has to face hostility in its community, and so he exhorts the church to stand firm for the faith of the gospel (1:27-30). Although martyrdom was a distinct possibility for both Paul and his readers, he encourages them to be unmovable, since in the end Christ and his cause will triumph.

Also, Paul is concerned about divisions within the ranks of the church. There is no reason to believe that doctrinal disputes were threatening to tear the church apart, however, personal differences threatened to fracture the unity the believers had in Christ. For that reason he warns against rivalry, selfishness and animosity, which are more often than not the causes of disunity. He even mentions several leading women by name, exhorting them to put aside their differences and work together in harmony (2:2-4; 4:2).

Chapter 3 is largely a warning against false teachings. Whether the opponents of the Philippians, mentioned in 1:28, were the same as those referred to in chapter 3 is not certain, but Paul has some very harsh things to say about the enemies of the Christian faith in this chapter. Paul calls them "dogs" and "evil workers" (3:2). It looks as if they were trying to force the practice of circumcision upon Gentile believers. "Beware of those who mutilate the flesh" (3:2). It looks as if unbelieving Jews, perhaps coming from Thessalonica who were not persuaded by the gospel, were creating problems for the Philippians. Paul argues that a righteousness that is achieved by human effort does not stand up before God.

At the end of the chapter he writes with tears about those who have become the enemies of the cross. Some think Paul has a different group of opponents in mind at this point, namely, libertines who went to the opposite extreme of the Jewish legalists. However, these may in fact be the same false teachers to whom he spoke so harshly at the beginning of the chapter.

C. The Place of Origin.

Where did Paul write this letter to the Philippians? From the letter itself we learn only that Paul was in prison and his case was to be decided shortly. He does not know whether the verdict will be in his favor or not and he is prepared to die. But he is also willing to continue on earth to serve his Master and the church.

Perhaps it is helpful if we briefly trace Paul's movements in the years just previous to the writing of this letter. In the closing years of his Aegean ministry, the apostle had arranged for a collection in the Gentile churches which was to be taken to the poor Christians of Judea. He arrived in Jerusalem in A.D. 57 and handed over these contributions of the churches to the leaders of the mother church. Shortly thereafter he was attacked by a hostile mob in the temple and he barely escaped with his life. Thanks to the Roman garrison in the Antonia Fortress he was rescued, taken into custody and sent to the procurator Felix at Caesarea on the coast (Acts 22-23).

In Caesarea Paul languished in prison for two years (A.D. 57-59), waiting for Felix to make a decision in his case (Acts 24:26,27). Felix, however, dragged his feet (hoping to receive a bribe) and left Paul in prison when his tenure as governor came to an end. His successor Festus did not seem to be in any hurry either to dispose of Paul's case, and so Paul availed himself of his right as a Roman citizen and appealed to Caesar. This meant he had to be sent to Rome.

Paul arrived in Rome after a treacherous sea voyage in A.D. 60 and was put under house arrest, waiting for his case to be heard by Nero or his deputy (Acts 27-28). Traditionally it was thought it was in Rome that Paul received the gifts of the Philippians through Epaphroditus and he wrote the letter to them, sending it along with Epaphroditus when he returned home. However, at least two other places of imprisonment have been suggested as possible places, where Paul wrote this letter.

Some scholars have suggested Ephesus as the point of origin of this letter. Paul did serve in Ephesus for several years and in the end a riot broke out (Acts 19). It is assumed that Paul must have spent some time in prison in Ephesus, although this is nowhere explicitly stated. One of the main reasons Ephesus is preferred over Rome as the source of the Philippian letter is its proximity to Philippi. Travel between Rome and Philippi could take as long as a month. If we assume that Rome is the place of origin, then we must allow time for the Philippians to hear of Paul's imprisonment in Rome. Epaphroditus then traveled to Rome, bringing the gifts of the Philippians. Then the news that

their representative had fallen ill had come to Philippi. Also, Epaphroditus had heard of the Philippians' anxiety at the news of his illness. And, as Paul wrote this letter, Epaphroditus was about to return
home. All this took time. However, Paul spent two years in Rome
before his case was heard and so there seems to have been plenty of
time for all these journeys back and forth to have taken place.

It has been pointed out that Paul planned to go to Spain after visiting Rome, whereas in this letter he plans to come to Philippi, and so he
must be writing from some place other than Rome. However, Paul's
situation had changed since he wrote about his future plans in his letter to the Romans. At that time he was still free; now he is a prisoner,
and so his hopes of going farther west are not an option at the moment.

He did spend two years in prison in Caesarea before he came to
Rome, and theoretically it is possible he wrote to the Philippians
from there, although this is an even more unlikely place of origin
than Ephesus. When Paul says "the whole palace guard and all the
others here know that I am in prison because I am a servant of
Christ" (1:13), the reference seems to be to an imprisonment in Rome.
However, it is possible the Greek word *praitorion* (Latin: *praetorium)*
is a reference to the headquarters of a proconsul or the seat of the
governor in Caesarea (Acts 23:3 5).

More problematic is the reference to the "saints . . . of Caesar's
household" (4:22) if we argue for Ephesus or Caesarea as the place of
origin. Although the imperial service in the province could possibly
be called members of Caesar's household, it is more likely there
should be Christians in Caesar's household in Rome. Also, Paul's reference to the progress of the gospel, stimulated by his imprisonment
(1:12), would appear to fit a Roman imprisonment better. Assuming
that Paul wrote this letter from Rome, its date falls into the two-year
period of A.D. 60-62.

D. The Author.

Philippians has generally been accepted as a genuine letter of Paul.
The letter claims to come from Paul and that claim has rarely been
challenged. The picture of Paul that emerges from this letter is of the
same Paul we meet in his other letters. The vocabulary Paul uses in
Philippians resembles that of his other letters, apart from some of the

words in that great hymnic passage in 2:6-11.

Apparently there was never any serious doubt about the Pauline authorship of this letter among the early church Fathers, who quote Philippians and assign the letter to Paul. Philippians also appears in the oldest extant canon lists which come from the second century. From time to time critics have expressed doubts about the Pauline authorship of Philippians, but very few Biblical scholars have followed them in this matter.

Paul begins his letter, as was the custom at that time, by mentioning his name. *Paulos* is the name the apostle bore in the Greco-Roman world in place of his Jewish name "Saul." Jews in the Hellenistic world often took on names that approximated the sound of their Hebrew and Aramaic names.

As on other occasions, Paul associates Timothy with himself in the salutation. However, Paul is the author of this letter, as can be seen from his use of the singular "I thank my God" (1:3). Perhaps Timothy is mentioned because he had shared in the planting of the church at Philippi. Also, by linking Timothy's name with his own, Paul may be saying that his colleague witnesses to the truths mentioned in this letter. He may even have been Paul's secretary to whom the apostle dictated his letter, although that cannot be said for certain.

Paul and Timothy are both called '"servants'" (literally "slaves") in the salutation. In addressing the Philippians, there was no need to remind them that he, Paul, was an apostle, for his authority was not challenged by his readers as it was in some other churches. To call himself and Timothy "slaves" of Jesus Christ may have shocked Greek hearers, for there is no record of this word being used to express religious devotion. But in the LXX (the Greek translation of the Hebrew Old Testament) the word is used to designate someone whom God used for a special ministry, people like Moses, Joshua, David, and others. And so one might see in the word "slaves" a title of honor. More likely, however, Paul uses the word in the ordinary Greek sense to underscore that he and Timothy were totally devoted to their Master Jesus Christ, and they were completely at his disposal.

E. The Character.

Philippians is a personal and friendly letter, frank and hearty in tone and somewhat artless in form. These characteristics become more obvious when one compares Philippians with Ephesians, for example, in which there are hardly any personal references at all. So full of personal references is Philippians that it has been called "Paul's Spiritual Autobiography" (Pickford 1949).

Although Paul writes under the most adverse circumstances, the letter bubbles with Christian joy. More than a dozen references to the word "joy" in some form or another can be found in this short epistle. Some think, in fact, that "joy" is the fundamental theme of the letter. Not even imprisonment could quench Paul's joy—a joy that is different from earthly joys which depend on pleasant circumstances.

We should, however, not think of this personal, friendly letter as a shallow piece of writing. There are passages, such as chapter 2:5-11, which certainly mock our sounding lines because of the profound depths of thought.

Because there is a change of tone in chapter 3, the unity of the epistle has been questioned. Some have speculated that Paul introduced a portion of another letter into the Philippian epistle in chapter 3. There is, of course, no manuscript evidence for such an insertion or addition. It is probably best to explain the change of mood simply in terms of the change of topics. When he writes about the dangers of the so called Judaizers, we expect Paul to write in a different vein from the one in which he addresses his friends in the church of Philippi. Sudden changes in tone are not uncommon in the letters of Paul.

From the expression in 3:1, that he is writing the same things to the Philippians, it has been argued that Paul must have written more than one letter to them. This view has found support in Polycarp's letter to the Philippians in which he mentions that Paul, when he was absent from Philippi, used to write letters to the Philippians. Also, in a Syriac canon list from the end of the fourth century, there is a reference to two letters of Paul to the Philippians. However, such references do not carry sufficient weight to be convincing. "To write the same things" is not necessarily a reference to other letters, but a repetition of certain themes in the same letter.

With these background remarks, let us now seek to read Paul's thoughts as he pens these lines from prison to his friends in Philippi.

Review Questions

1. *What led Paul and his companions to leave the Asiatic mainland and go to Europe?*

2. *What role did the Roman highways play in determining where Paul would go to start a new church?*

3. *How did Paul use his Roman citizenship to the advantage of the Philippians after he and Silas were released from prison?*

4. *Who were the first converts in Philippi?*

5. *Approximately how many years later did Paul write this letter to the Philippians?*

6. *What prompted the writing of this letter?*

7. *What are some of the pastoral concerns expressed in this letter?*

8. *The "word" joy is found throughout this letter from prison. What does that tell us about the meaning of Christian joy?*

CHAPTER TWO

Salutation and Thanksgiving (1:1-6)

*Paul and Timothy, servants of Christ Jesus, To all the saints
in Christ Jesus who are in Philippi, with the bishops and deacons: Grace to you and peace from God our Father and the Lord
Jesus Christ. I thank my God every time I remember you, constantly praying with joy in every one of my prayers for all of
you, because of your sharing in the gospel from the first day
until now. I am confident of this, that the one who began a good
work among you will bring it to completion by the day of Jesus
Christ (Philippians 1:1-6).*

It was custom in Paul's day to begin letters by mentioning the
author, the recipients, and to give a greeting. The edict of Nebuchadnezzar (Dan. 4:1) begins in similar fashion: "King Nebuchadnezzar to
all peoples . . . peace be multiplied to you.'" Letters in the Hellenistic
period were not too different from this oriental form. Although Paul
follows the literary pattern of his day in his letters, his salutations are
not stereotyped. He always takes his own circumstances and those of
his readers into account and makes appropriate adaptations. Besides

being creative in the way he opens his letters, he fills his prescripts with rich theological content. Since we have already spoken of Paul, the author of this letter, in our first chapter, we turn now to the addressees.

I. SALUTATION (vv. 1,2)

A. The Readers (v. 1)
    1. Their Designation. Paul uses the standard designation "saints" to address his Philippian readers. The background for this designation can be found in the Old Testament, where Israel is said to be a holy people. ("You shall be holy for I am holy", Lev. 11:4,5). To be holy means to be dedicated to God, to belong to him, to be at his service. To be holy does not mean people are without fault or they have reached a high point of perfection. It means they belong to God.

    People who belong to a holy God must, of course, avoid all that profanes, and so to be "saints" implies separation from evil. However, "saints" is not a designation of an elite group of believers who have attained to greater heights of holiness. It is a designation for all the members of the people of God, the church. As time went on, the designation "saints" came to be reserved for special groups of people within the Christian community, such as the martyrs, and so the word acquired a restricted meaning. But in the New Testament it is a word that designates all Christian believers.

    It is rather significant that the word "saints" (*hagioi* in Greek) is used regularly in the plural. The single saint, such as Saint Paul or Saint Peter, is not known in the early church. Titles such as "The Gospel According to Saint Mark," are additions of the later church. The plural "saints" suggests believers are found in community with one another. They don't live the Christian life in isolation, they are members of the church.

    2. Their Position. The believers in Philippi are said to be "in Christ Jesus." they are Christians (i.e., saints) not because of any merit on their own part but because they are in fellowship with Christ. To say the readers are "in Christ" is not too different from saying they are members of the body of Christ. It means they are in union with Christ; they share his life. The phrase "in Christ" could be thought of as the sphere in which the believers live. It is a popular phrase in Paul's letters and it occurs 164 times, not counting the pastoral epistles. In any case the phrase "in Christ Jesus" underscores the intimate relationship between the believer and the risen Christ. Just as Adam is seen as incorporating in himself the whole human race, so Christ, as it were, incorporates in himself a new humanity: his people, the church.

    3. Their Location. If "in Christ Jesus" speaks of the spiritual realm in which the Philippian believers lived and had their being, then "in Philippi" locates them geographically. The "saints" to whom Paul addresses this letter have not yet reached their heavenly destination. They are still on this earth; they live in Philippi. Although their true citizenship is in heaven (3:20), they are at home here on earth. They labor and toil at earthly tasks; they are beset by human weakness'; they are tempted by the evils surrounding them in Philippi; they suffer opposition from those who reject God and the gospel of Jesus Christ.

    Paul was a city missionary. He left it up to his converts in the cities to spread the gospel to the surrounding countryside. He was convinced it was possible for believers to live the Christian life in cities. In the past the city has sometimes been viewed as the bastion of iniquity (and who is to say it is not), which believers should avoid. Granted it is not always easy to walk the Christian way in hostile anti-Christian surroundings, Paul was confident that one could be a "saint" even in Philippi. In Revelation 2:13 our Lord comforts the church at Pergamum with the words "I know where you live."

    It may be of interest to point out that the churches of the first century are designated simply by their geographical location. There were as yet no denominational labels that are nowadays attached to churches. Nor do we know of any descriptive titles (or non-descriptive, such as "community church"). We are simply told where they are located.

    4. Their Leaders. "To all the saints in Christ Jesus who are in Philippi, with the bishops and deacons." Paul also greets the spiritual leaders of the church, namely the bishops and deacons. There was no one official designation of church leaders in New Testament times. They have a variety of names: elders, pastors (i.e., shepherds), teachers or simply "those who work among you, who guide and instruct you in the Christian life" (I Thess. 5:12). Here they are called bishops *(episkopoi)* . The word means to oversee, to inspect, to watch over. It was not originally a religious word, but was used in everyday life for watchmen, army officers or superintendents. However, the word was recast and came to be used specifically for leaders of the church who watched over and cared for the members of the congregation.

It is important that the word is regularly used in the plural, for in the early church the spiritual leaders were chosen from the local congregation and we have what has come to be called a "multiple ministry." The monepiscopate is a concept that belongs to a somewhat later period of church history. No doubt when a local congregation chose several men to instruct, to care for and to watch over the members of the church, one of them would act as chairman, but such details are not given on the pages of the New Testament. Also, we do not find that rather sharp distinction between clergy and laity in the early church that has so often characterized churches of later periods. From Paul's address to the Ephesian elders (Acts 20:17) we can see "elders" is a term used interchangeably with "bishops" or "pastors" (Acts 20:28).

Together with the "overseers" Paul mentions the "deacons." The word itself *(diakonoi)* means simply "servants." To begin with the word designated any kind of service, such as waiting at tables. In the New Testament the word is ennobled in that it is used to describe service that God's children perform in Christ's name. Christ called himself *diakonos* and taught his followers that in order to be truly great one needed to be a servant (Mk.10:44,45). Eventually the word *diakonos* took on a kind of technical meaning to describe those leaders of the church who served its members in a variety of ways. Taking Acts 6 as prototype, deacons have often been thought of as ministering to the physical and material needs of the church, in contrast to elders or bishops who focused on the church's spiritual needs. However, that is probably too narrow a definition of the ministry of deacons. In our welfare societies deacons today often feel like "displaced" persons, but surely there are always needs in a congregation that are not met by the welfare systems of the state.

B. The Greeting (v. 2)

"Grace to you and peace from God our Father and the Lord Jesus Christ."

1. The Content of the Greeting. Grace and Peace. It looks as if Paul combined the conventional greetings of both Greeks and Jews in his greetings to his readers. Greeks might greet each other with "joy" (*chairein*), and that word is found in secular letters (e.g., in the letter of Claudius Lysias to Felix in Acts 23:26), as well as in Christian greetings (such as Jam. 1:1).

With a minor linguistic shift Paul greets his readers with "grace" (*charis*). The word grace is found 144 times in the New Testament and is a key to Pauline theology (he uses it about 100 times). The word itself can mean simply charm or beauty (as can be seen in our English "gracious" or "graceful"). Sometimes the word grace describes a gift or simply generosity, as well as the response to some gift. "To have grace" is a Greek idiom for thanksgiving. However, in the New Testament it more often than not designates the undeserved love and mercy of God, manifested in Christ to a lost and sinful humanity.

Grace and peace may be viewed as shorthand for all the blessings of salvation that have come to us freely in Christ. In the Semitic world the common everyday greeting was "peace" (*shalom*), as it is to this day. Paul takes the greeting of the West and the East, as it were, and baptizes them into Christ and thereby deepens the meaning of these two words. Peace means not only tranquillity and harmony but wholeness, well-being and, above all, salvation. These two words, grace and peace, sum up all the gifts of God in Christ. They express the essence of the gospel; they form a kind of benediction on Paul's readers. We have heard them so often they have become commonplace, but in Paul's day the readers were probably quite overwhelmed when they heard these words of greeting for the first time.

2. The Source of the Greeting. "From God our Father and the Lord Jesus Christ." Although it is Paul who wishes them grace and peace, he knows the true source of these benedictions is in God. And through Jesus Christ, the God of Abraham, Isaac and Jacob has become the Father of the new people of God, the church. Although God is called "Father" even in the Old Testament, the word is used in the sense that he is the Creator of all humankind and especially the

Creator of Israel as his people. Through the coming of Jesus, however, God was revealed to us as Father in a new way. He even taught
us to pray "Abba," something Jews would have thought to be too
intimate.

With God the Father Paul mentions "the Lord Jesus Christ." The
pronoun "our" should be read with both "God" and "the Lord Jesus
Christ." It adds a touch of personal intimacy. Paul has no inhibitions
about mentioning Christ in the same breath that he says "God," since
for him Christ is divine, and so he can put him on the same level as
God. It would have been hard for a monotheistic Jew, like Paul, to put
God and Christ on the same level had the apostle not been convinced
that Christ partook of the nature of deity.

Repeatedly one finds in the letters of Paul the full title "the Lord
Jesus Christ." Jesus was a common Jewish name and is simply the
Greek form of the name Joshua. It was the name given to the earthly
Jesus by the angel of God (Mt. 1:21). "Christ" *(christos)* is the Greek
translation of the Hebrew "messiah" and means "the anointed one."
To be anointed meant someone was chosen and equipped by God to
carry out a particular mission. Jesus was uniquely anointed by God
to be the Saviour of all humankind. The title "Lord" (*kurios)* was frequently used as the Greek translation of the Hebrew name for God
(Yahweh) in the Septuagint version (the earliest Greek translation of
the Hebrew Bible). It was also used to address kings and emperors as
well as the masters of slaves, and sometimes it meant no more than
"sir." However, when Paul calls Jesus "Lord," he acknowledges him
as the one who by his death and resurrection was exalted by God far
above all human authorities. When people acknowledge Christ as
Lord, says Paul (Rom. 10:9,10), they are saved. That means more than
simply to say the word "Lord," and Paul reminds us that the confession of Jesus as Lord can be made only by the help of the Holy Spirit
(I Cor. 12:3).

We may wish each other a good day a hundred times but cannot
make it good by ourselves. But when Paul greets his readers with
grace and peace that come from God the Father and the Lord Jesus
Christ, he knows these wonderful benedictions are available to his
readers in Philippi, and his prayer is they might experience these at
an even deeper level than they had initially experienced them.

II. THE THANKSGIVING (vv. 3-6)

Paul regularly follows the prescript of his letters, with an introductory thanksgiving (Galatians is an exception). In this respect also he follows the letter style of his day. From the second century A.D. comes a letter which has close parallels to the letters of Paul: "Apion to Epimachos his father and lord, very many greetings . . . I thank the Lord Serapis" (Barrett, *The New Testament Background*, pp. 27-29).

A. The Address (v. 3a)

"I thank my God." Paul stands alone before God. Timothy, who is named in the salutation, is not mentioned now. We sense the personal and vital relationship between Paul and his God. And just as in the case of the greeting, the apostle takes the customary convention of beginning a letter with a thanksgiving and makes it express the intensity of his devotion to God and his tender feelings for his friends.

This is not a community thanksgiving but a private expression of gratitude toward a God whom he has come to know personally. The word for "thank" is the Greek *eucharisteo* and is somewhat broader in meaning than the English expression "to give thanks." In English "thank you" normally denotes the expression of gratitude for some personal benefit received, but here Paul uses the word in the sense of "praise."

B. The Occasion (vv. 3b,4)

"I thank my God every time I remember you." The meaning seems to be that Paul thanked God for the Philippians whenever he remembered them in his prayers. "Constantly praying with joy in every one of my prayers for all of you" (v. 4). Others think the meaning is rather that Paul thanked God for his readers everytime he even thought of them.

Be that as it may, Paul not only thanked God but also prayed to God for them. The word "constantly" should not be understood as if Paul did nothing else but thank and pray, but rather that Paul did not forget the Philippians in his prayers. Four times in succession Paul uses some form of the word "all." The alliteration in Greek cannot be reproduced in translation.

Again Paul's prayer for his readers is intensely personal ("my prayer"). It is also constant ("always") and it is inclusive ("for all of you"). Did he mention them by name? Surely by now he would not have known all the members of the church by name. Perhaps he mentioned specific needs of which he was aware when he prayed to God. That he made specific requests when he prayed is suggested by the word *deesis*, which is not the general word for prayer but means "petition." To pray for people specifically or for specific needs makes intercessory prayer vital.

It is also important to notice that Paul does not look upon his prayers for his friends as an arduous task that has to be performed. He makes his prayers, so he says, "with joy." Here we have the first reference to joy which is a note that will be struck many times throughout the letter.

Joy in the New Testament is not so much a mood or an emotion as it is a confident way of looking at life. Moods are determined by any number of circumstances, but Christian joy can encompass both elation and depression, success and tragedy. It is an inner peace that comes from confidence in God and his grace. It is the chuckle of the soul, one might say; eschatological joy, for it looks at the trammels of our earthly existence from the standpoint of the future, which is bright and glorious.

C. The Encouragement (vv. 5,6)
1. The Fellowship of the Readers (v. 5). "Because of your sharing in the gospel from the first day until now." Paul is encouraged to give thanks to God when he prays for the Philippians because of their *koinonia* (partnership) in the gospel. The word *koinonia* means to share, to have in common. Of the nineteen times that the word occurs in the New Testament, thirteen of its occurrences are in the Pauline writings.

Fellowship, partnership or sharing in the gospel could be understood to mean that Paul's converts had shared in the benefits of the gospel when they put their trust in Christ, and this they did. However, the context suggests the fellowship in the gospel here means they shared with the apostle in the great work of spreading the gospel. The suggestion that they shared with Paul in the ongoing work of the gospel by sending him monetary help is too limited an understanding of "gospel fellowship." "Koinonia" in the gospel would include giving of one's material means to support God's messengers, but in the case of the Philippians they did more than contribute money for evangelism; they participated also in spreading the good news in their city.

The word "gospel" (*euangelion*) is a favorite word of Paul. Used in its secular sense, it meant any kind of good news. In the New Testament, however, it is used in a special way to designate the good news that God in Christ has redeemed the world and offers all humankind forgiveness and deliverance from sin and death. To begin with *euangelion* was spoken, proclaimed and heard good news. Eventually several apostolic writers put the good news to writing, and we now call their books "Gospels."

The participation of the Philippians in the ongoing work of evangelism was not a fleeting or momentary outburst of enthusiasm. "From the first day until now" suggests that this church took its mission seriously. For example, they had contributed to Paul's mission at the beginning, and now again ten years later.

2. The Faithfulness of God (v. 6). "I am confident of this, that the one who began a good work among you will bring it to completion by the day of Jesus Christ." Paul is grateful when he prays, not only for what the Philippian readers are doing, but particularly for what God is doing in their lives. It should be said, however, that their achievements in the work of the kingdom were also fruits of God's grace and power in their lives.

Although the name "God" does not appear in this verse, clearly Paul's confidence is in God. He describes God as the one who began and will complete the good work in the Philippians. The good work which God began in the lives of the readers has been understood by some to be a back-reference to their participation in the spread of the gospel, including their monetary gifts. This was no doubt a good work, but the context demands we understand "good work" as a reference to God's work of redemption which the Philippians experienced when they first believed.

Salvation, however, is not only an initial experience but is ongoing, and so Paul expresses confidence that the God who began the good

work in their lives will bring it to completion on the day of Jesus
Christ. The day of Jesus Christ is the day of his return at the end of
the age. It is just one of a number of ways in which this last day is
designated.   This is a word of great assurance and consolation to
those who are fearful or are sometimes plagued with doubts. Our salvation is not something we can attain to in our own strength. We
must leave it to God; and God, Paul assures us, will not leave unfinished what he begins.

Perhaps another inference may be made. As long as we are on this
earth, in this body, we cannot attain perfection. We have limitations
and failures; we suffer from sickness and tragedy, and some day we
must die. And so we should be modest in all our claims about our
experiences of God's grace and power. God's power is made perfect
in weakness. God is the First and the Last; when Christ returns we
shall enter the gates of perfection.

Review Questions

1. *Why are believers in the New Testament called "saints?"*

2. *What do you think are the duties of elders and deacons today?*

3. *What are some of the meanings of the word "peace?"*

4. *How would the confession that Jesus is Lord express itself in our lives
today?*

5. *What can we learn about intercessory prayer from our passage?*

6. *How would "fellowship in the gospel" express itself in our situation?*

7. *Does the assurance that God will complete what he has begun in our lives
relieve us of all responsibility?*

CHAPTER THREE

Praying For Christian Friends (1: 7-11)

It is right for me to think this way about all of you, because you hold me in your heart, for all of you share in God's grace with me, both in my imprisonment and in the defense and confirmation of the gospel. For God is my witness, how I long for all of you with the compassion of Christ Jesus. And this is my prayer, that your love may overflow more and more with knowledge and full insight to help you to determine what is best, so that in the day of Christ you may be pure and blameless, having produced the harvest of righteousness that comes through Jesus Christ for the glory and praise of God (Philippians 1: 7-11).

Paul has already assured his friends of his prayers on their behalf (v. 4). He will now become more specific and tell his readers what he prays for. One might call it a "prayer report." Since love is of the very essence of the Christian life it should not surprise us that Paul prays for an increase in love. The apostle was deeply convinced that only God could sustain the churches which he had planted and bring them to spiritual maturity. For this reason he gave himself constantly

to the ministry of intercession for his converts. Perhaps there is nothing that expresses our love and concern for others as clearly as do our
supplications on their behalf. Intercessory prayers are selfless
prayers. When we intercede for others in the name of Jesus we
implore God to lay his hand of blessing on the people we are praying for. And in this respect Paul is an outstanding model for us.
Before he informs his readers about his supplications for them, he
assures them of his genuine affection for them (vv. 7,8). Philippians
has rightfully been called a "model of friendship."

I. PAUL'S FEELINGS FOR HIS READERS (vv. 7,8)

A. His Appreciation for Them (v. 7a)
"It is right for me to think this way about all of you." Paul wants
all of them to know it is only natural that he should feel about them
as he does. Did Paul suspect that some of the Philippians might think
he had gone too far in his praise of the church and for that reason had
to assure them that his estimate of them was entirely proper? We do
not know but it is quite possible.

The verb *phroneo* can mean to think, to feel, to be disposed, to be
concerned. It is right and proper for Paul to be "minded" as he is
"because you hold me in your heart." Or is it "because I hold you in
my heart?" Grammatically either translation is possible and in everyday life affection is usually reciprocal; it is not a one-way street. Since
he calls on God to be witness to his affection for them (v. 8), it may be
best to understand Paul to say it is only right for him to feel so kindly
toward his readers because he has them in his heart.

The "heart" is used here in its customary Old Testament sense as the
seat of emotion, affection, thought and will. It is the seat of physical,
mental and spiritual life. To hold someone in his or her heart means that
such a person is very dear to an individual. When one recalls that Paul
used to be a Pharisee who was meticulous about keeping himself free
from defilement by contact with non-Jews, one is amazed at how God's
love has broken down all barriers and the apostle is free to express his
affection for these young believers, most of whom were Gentiles.

B. His Association with Them (v. 7b)

"For all of you share in God's grace with me, both in my imprisonment and in the defense and confirmation of the gospel." For the second time in these opening verses (see v. 5) the Philippians are said to "share" with Paul. They are "fellowsharers" of God's grace. "Grace" in this context is probably not a reference to the saving grace of God, but rather to the calling of Paul to be an apostle, the call to proclaim the gospel (cf. Rom. 1:5; 12:3,6; 1 Cor. 3:10; Gal. 2:9; Eph. 3:2). Grace speaks of the special gift given to Paul to accomplish his missionary task. And the readers shared in this by contributing to Paul's ministry.

This calling to proclaim the gospel brought Paul into prison. For the first time in this letter the apostle makes it clear he is a prisoner. How did the readers share in his imprisonment? Obviously they were not in prison also. Rather, they did what they could do to alleviate Paul's sufferings in prison.

And even in prison Paul continued to witness. He speaks of his "defense and confirmation of the gospel" as a prisoner. We know that while he was under house arrest he taught those who came to him (Acts 28:31). Soon he will stand before a Roman judge and will have to defend himself. This would provide him with another occasion to expound the good news of the gospel. He had already done this earlier before Felix and Festus. And the Philippians, by standing by Paul with their gifts and prayers, were sharing with him in the establishment of the gospel message. It may even be he had already defended himself before a Roman judge and in the process explained the gospel which he preached, and now he was awaiting the verdict.

C. His Attachment to Them (v. 8)

"For God is my witness, how I long for all of you with the compassion of Christ Jesus." Why does Paul use such strong language? Is he saying he yearns for them with profound affection but cannot express his feelings adequately in words, and so points to God as his witness? It may be there were those in the church who were not so convinced of Paul's love for them. No doubt Paul knew about Jesus' prohibition of oathmaking (Mt. 5:34-37) and must have felt that to call on God as his witness was not a violation of that proscription. So intense are his feelings of affection for his readers that he can only say "God knows."

Paul has an intense yearning to be reunited with the congregation. He longs to see them again. Repeatedly Paul uses the word "to long for" when expressing his affection for his friends (Rom. 1:11; I Thess. 3:6; 2 Tim. 1:4). But it is a longing that is not only intense but really quite unique. Literally he longs for them "in the viscera of Christ Jesus." In Greek the viscera (*ta splagchna*) were the nobler organs of the body, such as heart, liver and lungs, and were regarded as the seat of tender emotions. The word is used very much as we use the word "heart." In older English versions the word *splagchna* was translated as "bowels" but that rendering is completely obsolete. Paul longs for the church with Christ's "inward parts," i.e., Christ's heart. He loves them the way Christ loves them. "Loving you as Christ loves you" (JB).

II. PAUL'S PRAYER FOR THE READERS (vv. 9-11)

A. The Contents of the Prayer (v. 9)

"And this is my prayer, that your love may overflow more and more with knowledge and full insight." That Paul prayed for the church has already been stated (see v. 4), but now we discover what Paul prays for. Briefly stated, he prays for an increase in love.

Love (*agape*) is the chief characteristic of the Christian life (see I Cor. 13). The object of love is omitted here. Paul does not say whether it is love for the unbeliever, for the believer, for himself personally or for God that is in need of growth. Perhaps these are all so interrelated that one does not need to ask the question: love for whom? Love is the most comprehensive and fundamental element of the life of a believer.

Paul's prayer is for growth in love. Literally he prays that their love "overflow (*perisseuo*) more and more." The verb means to superabound, to manifest abundance. No one ever comes to the point in his or her Christian life where growth in love is no longer possible. *Agape* has little to do with warm feelings but more with the will and with attitudes. Love for others shows itself in deeds and there are no limits to growth in this area.

This love, Paul hopes, will be accompanied by true knowledge and perception. It is not a foolish infatuation that gushes out in wild profusion, but a love that is guided by discernment. One could read the text to mean that by knowledge and perception love would grow and overflow. Deeper spiritual insights and delicate sensitivity for what is appropriate could be seen as the means of growth in love. On the other hand, full knowledge (*epignosis*) and spiritual insight (*aisthesis* - our word "aesthetic") may indicate the manner in which an increase in love manifests itself. As our love increases we become more perceptive; we learn to express our love for others in more appropriate ways.

One could also view "knowledge" and "discernment" as the two banks in which the river of love flows. Love is discriminating; it is not to be equated with easygoing tolerance. Love can also have a stern quality about it; "it rejoices with the truth" (I Cor. 13:6). Love for others does not overlook moral issues—the need for holiness, uprightness and truth.

Paul's prayer should not be understood as a rebuke of the Philippians. The love of God had been poured in their hearts by the Holy Spirit (Rom. 5:5). But love is open to unlimited growth, and to grow in love is to live "the abundant life."

B. The Purport of the Prayer (v. 10a)

"To help you to determine what is best." True knowledge and spiritual sensitivity will enable the Philippians to be more discerning. Although grammatically this could be classified as a purpose clause, it seems best to speak of it as the consequence of growth in love. For that reason we call it the purport of prayer.

Repeatedly Paul mentions the need for discernment in the Christian life. Spiritually mature believers are able to "distinguish between good and evil" (Heb. 5:14). Our text speaks of discernment on an even higher plane: to discern and choose what is best. The word "discern" (*dokimazo*) means to examine, to put to the test, and then to approve. It was employed, for example, for the testing of metals and money. That which passes the test stands approved, and that is the meaning in our text: to approve what is best.

The verb *diaphero* basically means to go in two directions, hence to differ. In our passage it signifies the things which excel, things which differ by surpassing others. To distinguish between the good and the better is a step beyond distinguishing between right and wrong; it means to choose what is best. "That small things should as small be seen, and great things great to us should seem" is a good motto for the believer in everyday life. Many things in life have no real value, and we must not foolishly spend our time and talents on them. In a time in which there is such a confusion of values, Christians need an extra measure of grace to be able to discern and   approve those things which please God and contribute to the ongoing work of his kingdom.

C. The Purpose of the Prayer (v. 10b)

"So that in the day of Christ you may be pure and blameless." The etymology of the word *eilikrines* (pure) is not certain, but it appears to be derived from the word *heile* (*helios* is the Greek word for "sun")— a word suggesting warmth and light, and *krino* is "to judge." If this is so, then the picture is that of something being examined in the sunlight. Recently I bought a suit and the clerk asked me whether I would care to step outside the store for a moment to see what it looked like in the sunlight. In any case, through usage the word has come to mean sincere, pure and spotless. Here, of course, it is used not in a physical sense but the moral sense. Paul prays that through an increase in love, sensitivity and discernment, his readers will become people whose lives are transparent before God and other people.

The other adjective (*aproskopos*) literally means not stumbling or not causing others to stumble. In its ethical sense it signifies a person who seeks to avoid everything that would cause another person to trip and fall. Paul wants his readers to be without offense toward their brothers and sisters in the church as well as to unbelievers. To be free from all impurity and blame is a goal no person in his or her own strength can achieve, and so Paul implores God in his prayers that he might accomplish this in the lives of the Philippians.

This kind of life prepares believers for the Day of Christ. That last day when Christ returns will be a day of scrutiny, and so the thought of Christ's coming adds a seriousness to Christian ethics. A similar thought is expressed in I Thessalonians 5:23, where Paul prays that God might keep his readers "free from every fault at the coming of our Lord Jesus Christ." This is the second mention of the return of Christ in these introductory verses (see v. 6). Paul not only wants the Philippians to be present on that last day, but he wants them to be pleasing to God when they stand before the judgement seat of Christ (2 Cor. 5:10).

D. The Hope of the Prayer (v. 11)

"Having produced the harvest of righteousness that comes through Jesus Christ for the glory and praise of God." At the conclusion of his intercessory prayer Paul expresses the hope that they will not only be accepted by God on that last day, but they will be filled with fruit that comes from a right relationship with God. "Fruit of righteousness" is a reference to the harvest of godly qualities such as love, joy, peace, etc. (Gal. 5:22—there called "the fruit of the Spirit"). Paul does not want his readers to appear impoverished at the gates of heaven, but wants them to bear a full crop of righteous deeds and actions— "truly good qualities" as the Good News Bible has it.

Such a crop or harvest of goodness is not self-generated but comes only through Jesus Christ. The fruit of a right relationship with God rules out all self-congratulation. Indeed Paul closes with a doxology: "for the glory and praise of God." "Glory" is used here very much in the sense of "praise." Doxologies were frequently used at the conclusion of Old Testament and Jewish prayers (e.g., Ps. 21:13; 35:28; 41:13). Here the doxology not only concludes Paul's prayer but it embraces his thanksgiving. This doxological note will be struck again in 2:11 and finally in 4:20 where it forms a grand finale to the letter.

Review Questions

1. *What can we learn from Paul's words of endearment in this letter?*

2. *How can we become "fellow-sharers" with those who are suffering for Christ's sake?*

3. *How might growth in love, for which Paul prays, manifest itself in daily life?*

4. *Is there a need for "discernment" in our expressions of love for others?*

5. *Give an illustration of how a person tests and then approves that which is best.*

6. *Will we ever be completely pure and blameless this side of heaven?*

7. *Sometimes fruitbearing is defined simply as soul-winning. How is it to be understood in our text, where Paul speaks of "fruit of righteousness?"*

CHAPTER FOUR

Honoring Christ in the Diversities of Life (1:12-26)

I want you to know, beloved , that what has happened to me has actually helped to spread the gospel, so that is has become known throughout the whole imperial guard and to everyone else that my imprisonment is for Christ; and most of the brothers and sisters, having been made confident in the Lord by my imprisonment, dare to speak the word with greater boldness and without fear. Some proclaim Christ from envy and rivalry, but others from goodwill. These proclaim Christ out of love, knowing that I have been put here for the defense of the gospel; the others proclaim Christ out of selfish ambition, not sincerely but intending to increase my suffering in my imprisonment. What does it matter? Just this, that Christ is proclaimed in every way, whether out of false motives or true; and in that I rejoice. Yes, and I will continue to rejoice, for I know that through your prayers and the help of the Spirit of Jesus Christ this will turn out for my deliverance. It is my eager expectation and hope that I will not be put to shame in any way, but that by my speaking with all boldness, Christ will be exalted now as always in my body, whether by life or by death. For to me, living is Christ and dying is gain. If I am to live in the flesh, that means fruitful

> *labor for me; and I do not know which I prefer. I am hard pressed*
> *between the two: my desire is to depart and be with Christ, for*
> *that is far better; but to remain in the flesh is more necessary for*
> *you. Since I am convinced of this, I know that I will remain and*
> *continue with all of you for your progress and joy in faith, so*
> *that I may share abundantly in your boasting in Christ Jesus*
> *when I come to you again (Philippians 1:12-26).*

For a good many years Paul had worked himself to the bone to bring the good news of God's redeeming love to the ends of the known world. In obedience to Christ's call on the Damascus Road, to bring the light of the gospel to those in darkness, he had traversed the lands of the Mediterranean world.

And now he lies in prison. From a human point of view that must have been a wrenching experience for an energetic missionary like Paul. Besides, he is suffering imprisonment innocently. He had committed no crime. And yet, we hear no complaints from his lips in the face of grave injustice and adversity. Paul had thatched his roof in good weather, and when the rains came and the winds beat upon his house, it stood firm, for it was built upon a rock. He has only one concern: that Christ be honored in his life, whether by life or by death. The following passage lets us in on the secret sources of Paul's indomitable faith.

I. VICTORIOUS IN SUFFERING (vv. 12-14)

A. The Affirmation (v. 12)

"I want you to know, beloved, that what has happened to me has actually helped to spread the gospel." The readers were deeply concerned about Paul; they knew he was in custody, awaiting a verdict from a Roman court. No doubt they thought it was a tragedy that the great apostle who had planted churches all over the empire should be condemned to imprisonment. Paul, however, looked at his lot from a higher vantage point and accepted adversity from the hand of God and humbly bowed to the Lord's will.

He assures the Philippians that "the things that happened" to him in fact contributed to the progress of the gospel. Instead of complaining about his miserable circumstances—his clothes, his food, his lack of freedom—he wants his brothers and sisters to know the gospel is making headway. The word *prokope* (advance) means quite literally to cut ahead, to remove barriers. Although Paul is in bonds, the word of God is not bound (2 Tim. 2:9).

While under house arrest he had many visitors (Acts 28) and this gave him an opportunity to spread the good news. Also, he would soon appear (or did he already have his day in court?) before the supreme court of Rome, and that would give him another opportunity to explain to the Roman authorities what it was that he believed and proclaimed.

God's ways are past finding out and Paul did not always understand God's mysterious leading in his life, but he had the confidence that as he submitted his life to the will of God, God would be honored even in the midst of adversities.

B. The Explanation (v. 13)

"So that it has become known throughout the whole imperial guard and to everyone else that my imprisonment is for Christ." This is Paul's explanation of his claim, that his incarceration had led to the spread of the gospel. Literally his bonds in Christ have become manifest. From this statement some have inferred that his trials had already taken place and he was awaiting the judge's verdict. In any case, it has become clear that Paul is in prison because of his faith in Christ. He is a prisoner not because he had committed a crime but because of his Christian faith. Rome was quite tolerant of other religions at this time, and the rumor that Paul was put in prison because of his faith must have spread widely.

It had become known in the entire *praetorium* that a man had been imprisoned because of his faith. *Praitorion* is a Greek word derived from the Latin *praetorium*, which originally referred to the officer's tent in a military camp. Eventually it was used also for the official residence of a governor. Precisely what meaning it has in our text is not altogether clear. It could be the emperor's palace in Rome or the military barracks attached to the imperial residence. Most scholars today hold that it refers not to a place but to those people who formed the praetorian guard.

What is meant with "and all the rest" is not clear either. Does Paul mean that besides the praetorian guard, the public at large knows why he is in captivity (so the New English Bible suggests)? It could also refer to the church in the city, as the next verse might suggest.

C. The Encouragement (v. 14)

"And most of the brothers and sisters having been made confident in the Lord by my imprisonment, dare to speak the word with greater boldness and without fear." Paul's captivity not only advanced the cause of the gospel in the non-Christian community, it had a positive effect on the members of the Roman church as well. It had given Christian believers in the imperial city greater courage to speak the word without fear. When Paul was brought to Rome as a prisoner because of his faith, they may have shrunk back, fearing that what happened to Paul might also happen to them. But Paul's witness while in prison gave them boldness as well.

"To speak the word" is shorthand for spreading the word of God (in fact there is a variant reading that has "word of God"). Sometimes it is called "the word of the Lord" or "the word of salvation" or "the word of the cross." But here it is simply "the word." The readers, of course, know it is God's word and not simply human words. There had been a renewal of ardor in spreading the good news of the gospel in the city, and Paul's example helped them to overcome fear and timidity.

II. TRIUMPH IN TRIALS (vv. 15-18)

A. The Trials (vv. 15-17)

"Some proclaim Christ from envy and rivalry, but others from goodwill. These proclaim Christ out of love, knowing that I have been put here for the defense of the gospel; the others proclaim Christ out of selfish ambition, not sincerely but intending to increase my suffering in my imprisonment."

Spiritual trials can be even more acute than physical adversity. Evidently there were Christians in Rome who were jealous of Paul whom God had chosen to spread the gospel all over the empire. For selfish reasons they were secretly glad that Paul was out of their way and they could now hold centre stage. It appears as if they wanted to rub salt into Paul's wounds by their ministry.

Paul does not condemn the message they were proclaiming. Evidently they were not preaching heresy. If they had been, Paul would have confronted them. But their motives were wrong. Motives were also important to Paul. One needs to read I Thessalonians 2:1-12 to discover what Paul thinks about wrong motives in Christian service. However, in the current situation Paul is facing a personal attack and so he will not react with anger.

Fortunately there were still those who proclaimed Christ out of love and goodwill. They knew Paul was suffering for the sake of the gospel of Christ and that he was faithfully defending the gospel. They were not embarrassed or put off by his imprisonment, but rather they identified with him.

The rival group thought they could stir up more trouble for Paul by their preaching, perhaps by reminding him of his restraints compared to their freedom. It was a case of petty rivalry, it seems, or of complete misunderstanding of suffering and adversity in the lives of God's servants. They may have thought that by forging ahead with the spread of the gospel they would add more pain to the physical misery Paul was already experiencing.

It is hard for us to imagine a situation like this, but it may be more common than we care to admit. Many a Christian has been wrecked through petty rivalry and jealousy.

B. The Triumph (v. 18)

"What does it matter? Just this, that Christ is proclaimed in every way, whether out of false motives or true: and in that I rejoice. Yes, and I will continue to rejoice." What then? asks Paul. Such being the case, how is he to respond to such annoyances? Well, it does not matter to him personally. He will not whine and complain because of attacks on his person. What really mattered, as far as Paul was concerned, was that Christ be proclaimed, whether out of false motives or with sincerity. To proclaim Christ is another way of designating the proclamation of the gospel, for Christ is the very heart of the gospel message.

Paul was a sensitive person and no doubt it hurt him to discover that people would proclaim Christ out of wrong motives and they should be so mean that they wanted to add to his trials. But he will not sink to their level and respond in kind. He triumphs over these attacks: "In this I rejoice and I will rejoice" that Christ is being proclaimed. His critics read their own immature behavior into Paul, but they fooled themselves. Instead of becoming bitter and attacking them, he expresses this joy at the spread of the gospel.

There were no verse divisions in Paul's letter to the Philippians and so it is not quite clear whether "And I will rejoice" belongs to Paul's triumph over the temptation to strike back at his critics, or whether it introduces the next paragraph in which he models for us the right Christian attitude in the face of adversity and uncertainty.

III. ASSURANCE IN UNCERTAINTY (vv. 19-26)

A. His Confidence (v. 19)

"For I know that through your prayers and the help of the Spirit of Jesus Christ this will turn out for my deliverance." Paul will soon get the verdict from the Roman supreme court. It could be life or death. Paul is on tenterhooks. But in spite of all this uncertainty, facing the possibility of a martyr's death, his words breathe assurance and confidence. "I know." What does he know? Had he heard rumors that the judgement in his case would be favorable? Sometimes he uses the word "perhaps" but here he says, "I know. "

Paul does not know whether he will be vindicated by Caesar's court or not, but he knows that ultimately he will be vindicated by God in the court of heaven. The language of our text is also found in Job 13:16 (LXX): "I know this will turn out for my salvation." Just what Paul meant by "salvation" is not quite clear. The word itself means deliverance, but the question is whether Paul had the confidence he would be delivered from prison or whether he is thinking of ultimate deliverance and vindication on the last day. Goodspeed makes it a bit too general when translated: "All this will turn out for my highest welfare."

The apostle could hardly have known he would be set free, even though he expresses the hope (v. 25) that he will have the opportunity once more to visit the Philippians. "I know" is a confession of faith; his life is in God's hands and whatever may happen, he knows that in the end he will be vindicated.

This triumphant outcome will be made possible, as he says, through the prayers of the Philippians and the Spirit of Jesus Christ. Earlier Paul mentioned his prayers for his readers; now he expects them to pray for him. The word for prayer (*deesis*) suggests a special request, a petition. And the apostle does not hesitate to place the prayers of these young Christians beside the Spirit of Jesus as the means which will affect his vindication. Paul believed firmly in the efficacy of prayer to change circumstances, and thereby he encourages us to pray about our daily tasks and troubles.

Paul is confident of the "supply" (*epichoregia*) of the Spirit of Jesus Christ. The Spirit of Jesus Christ is elsewhere called the Holy Spirit or the Spirit of God, or simply the Spirit. The etymology of the word "supply" is interesting. The Greek *choregeo* means literally "to lead a chorus." It was used also of money supplied by some patron for the training of a chorus, and so it comes to mean "abundant supply." Whether Paul means the Spirit will be supplied in rich measure or whether the Spirit will do the supplying is not quite clear, although the latter seems to be preferable. Jesus had promised his followers that the Spirit would help them, especially when they would have to stand before judges (Mk. 13:11; Mt. 10:20). Paul is confident the Spirit of the risen Christ will empower him to make a good confession.

Since prayer and the Spirit are mentioned together in our text, one is reminded of the passage in Romans 8:15ff where the Spirit is said to be our helper in our prayers, since we do not know what or how to pray as we ought.

B. His Concern (v. 20)

"It is my eager expectation and hope that I will not be put to shame in any way, but that by my speaking with all boldness, Christ will be exalted now as always in my body, whether by life or by death." While on one hand Paul is confident that he will be vindicated in the end, he also has concerns as long as he is in this body. Trust and confidence in God and his saving help does not mean Christians have no concerns or they are thereby insulated from the trials of life. Paul's concern, however, is not about personal safety or success or material prosperity, but rather about his manner of life and his witness to the gospel. He wants to glorify his Lord whether it be by life or death.

"My eager expectation" expresses Paul's longing in the midst of uncertainty and doubt. But, with the additional word "hope" one must say Paul's expectation is filled with confidence. "I passionately hope" (NEB) is expressed negatively first and then positively. Negatively he hopes he will not be put to shame.

The language here reminds us of the prayers of the Psalmists who often express the hope they will not be put to shame (LXX Ps. 24:3; 38:7; 118:80). Some think Paul means that when he will be released it will be obvious he is not a criminal and the gospel he preached is not a heresy. Others think Paul anticipates his trial at this point at which he will have to defend the gospel and his faith in Christ, and his hope is he will not be an embarrassment to his Lord. Still others feel Paul hopes to acquit himself in such a way that he will not have to be ashamed when Christ comes in glory (cf. I Jn. 2:28).

Stated positively the apostle wants to speak with boldness and exalt Christ, be it by life or death. The word "boldness" (*parrhesia*) means literally to say it all. In Greek democracy it meant freedom of speech. Between friends it describes the spirit of openness, the freedom to say what one wishes without fear of misunderstanding or incrimination. In the face of danger it can be translated as "boldness" or "courage." In the presence of God it speaks of confidence, especially in the matter of prayer.

In our text Paul expresses the hope that he will be bold in his testimony to his Lord and in that way he will make Christ great. The Greek verb *megaluno* means simply "to make great," "to magnify." To magnify is another way of saying he wants to "glorify" Christ. And he wants to do this with his whole being, although he mentions only his body. But that is because he is thinking of bodily life or death. Sometimes "body" stands for the person. "Now as always" is a phrase that suggests this desire of Paul to exalt his Lord is a constant concern of his.

Although the word "body" may be used in the sense of person, it should be added the body is the only instrument we have here on earth with which to glorify Christ. "You were bought with a price;

glorify God in your body," writes Paul to the Corinthians (I Cor. 6:20). That is a high view of the body. Our bodies are not to be viewed as ends in themselves but as means to an end.

Whether the court's verdict will be life or death is not even the greatest concern of Paul. He is concerned only with bringing honor to his Master. Surely this is not a Stoic indifference to life and death; rather it is the sublime indifference of a person whose life is in God's hands and who has submitted his entire being to the will of the heavenly Father. This complete consecration to God is seen even more clearly in the next verses .

C. His Consecration (vv. 21-24)

"For to me, living is Christ and dying is gain. If I am to live in the flesh, that means fruitful labor for me; and I do not know which I prefer. I am hard pressed between the two: my desire is to depart and to be with Christ, for that is far better; but to remain in the flesh is more necessary for you."

"For me to live is Christ." One can live in different ways, on different levels. There is biological existence or one can make life a concentrated pursuit of pleasure, power and possessions. But life can also be lived at a deeper level. Paul's life is Christ-centered. Christ gives meaning to his life; he is the source of his strength; he is his model in daily life. Everything that Paul does, trusts, hopes or possesses is inspired by Christ. After he was overwhelmed by Christ and his grace on his way to Damascus, the apostle can see no other reason for living but Christ.

That does not make his life trouble free. At the moment Paul is incarcerated; he suffers, he struggles, he is subject to attack by critics and enemies of the gospel. But even to die is gain and profit. How can death be profitable? Does he mean simply that with death he will be relieved of all his troubles? Or does he think a martyr's death would be gain for the ongoing work of the gospel here on earth, as it often was in the early centuries? Paul probably thinks of death as gain because of what follows death. If he dies he goes to be with Christ and that is much better than life here on earth.

As long as he is in the flesh he has prospects of fruitful labor, and so he is not quite sure whether he would prefer to die or continue to live. To live in the flesh means simply to exist in the body. Sometimes "flesh" has a pejorative meaning, but not here. Assuming for the moment that his trial leads to his release, he can anticipate work that is fruitful. The work he envisions must be the continuation of his missionary calling, and that gives his life meaning and purpose. And so with the hope of eternal life with Christ on one side of the scale, and the prospect of laboring in God's kingdom here on earth, on the other side, Paul hesitates to say which of the two he would choose. He will not tell us.

Since the choice before him is a genuine dilemma, the apostle feels "hemmed in on both sides." He is under pressure from both sides. Dying or living are the two horns of the dilemma which press in on Paul. On the one hand, he has a deep desire to depart and be with Christ. The word *analuo* (depart) was used to describe breaking up camp, pulling up the tent pegs, but also for the weighing of the anchor. The noun *analusis* (departure; our word "analysis") is used as a euphemism for death (2 Tim. 4:6), and the verb in our text also refers to death.

Whereas many people in our society cannot face either life or death, Paul embraced both. Death for him is not simply the separation of the soul from the body, but it means to be with Christ. The question is often asked: what happens to the believer who dies before the Lord returns, before the resurrection on the last day? Here is the answer: he or she goes to be with Christ. This is what in the language of theology is called "the intermediate state," since on the last day we shall receive the resurrection body.

Believers often wonder what it will be like when they leave this earth and enter into the presence of the Lord. If nothing more were said about this than what Paul says in our text, we could be satisfied. To be with Christ, he claims, is very much better. Paul heaps up comparatives to underscore that dying does not mean loss for the believer, but is great gain.

Although the prospect of being with Christ holds a great attraction for Paul, he does not want to be guided by personal desires. He considers the need of the Philippians and feels it is more necessary for him to remain in the flesh and be of service to them and other churches.

D. His Conviction (vv. 25,26)

"Since I am convinced of this, I know that I will remain and continue with all of you for the progress and joy of the faith, so that I may share abundantly in your boasting in Christ Jesus when I come to you again."

After expressing uncertainty about his future, we are rather surprised to hear Paul say so confidently that he will remain with all of them. Did Paul have a prophetic revelation as he wrote these lines, assuring him that he would be set free? Did he have some inside knowledge? Perhaps the emphasis lies more on the conviction that it is best for him to remain and be of help to the Philippians, than on the knowledge that he would be released. There is a play on words here (*meno*—to remain, and *parameno*—to stand by you). If God allows him to remain here on earth and he is set free from prison, he hopes "to stand by" his readers, in the sense that he will be of help and service to them.

His presence with them will lead to "progress and joy in the faith." Since the nouns progress and joy are joined by one article we could render them "joyful advance." "The faith" is used here absolutely to describe not a confession of faith in the sense of a system of theology or a doctrinal statement, but embraces the entire existence of the believers. Paul wants them to make progress in their Christian life— a progress that is attended by joy.

If this should happen, then there would be much "boasting in Christ Jesus." The grammar is abstruse at this point. Literally the text reads, "In order that your boasting may abound in Christ Jesus in me." Does that mean so that in me you may have ample cause to glory in Christ Jesus (so the Revised Standard Version)? Or "You will have another reason to give praise to Christ Jesus on my account" (Jerusalem Bible). Or "Your pride in me may be unbounded" (New English Bible).

The word "boast" is used here in the Old Testament sense, it seems: "Let him who boasts, boast in the Lord" (Jer. 9:24, LXX). It is not vain boasting, for it does not take place within the sphere of human ambition; that would be boasting in the flesh (2 Cor. 11:18). The ground for praising God will be that Paul has been set free and will come to the Philippians and help them.

Review Questions

1. *Can you think of an incident in your life in which God by his grace brought good out of adversity?*

2. *Is trouble in our lives the punishment for past misdeeds?*

3. *Did Paul always bear personal attacks silently? For a defence of his motives in preaching, see I Thessalonians 2:1-12.*

4. *If Paul could rejoice in prison and even when he was attacked, must we not revise our understanding of Christian joy?*

5. *How does a realistic view of death give depth to our life here on earth?*

6. *Where are our departed loved ones prior to the coming of Christ at the end of the age?*

7. *How does Christ give purpose and meaning to our work here on earth?*

CHAPTER FIVE

Worthy of the Gospel (1: 27-30)

Only, live your life in a manner worthy of the gospel of Christ, so that, whether I come and see you or am absent and hear about you, I will know that you are standing firm in one spirit, striving side by side with one mind for the faith of the gospel, and are in no way intimidated by your opponents. For them this is evidence of their destruction, but of your salvation. And this is God's doing. For he has graciously granted you the privilege not only of believing in Christ, but of suffering for him as well — since you are having the same struggle that you saw I had and now hear that I still have (Philippians 1:27-30).

There is little in this letter to indicate the Philippian church had any serious problems either in doctrine or in Christian deportment. However, Paul knew society looked upon those who had committed their lives to Jesus with a critical eye, and he didn't want his converts to give the enemies of the gospel an occasion to slander this young church.

That this continued to be an ongoing concern on the part of church leaders can be seen from a second century sermon, known as the "Second Letter of Clement." In it we read: "For the Gentiles when they hear from our mouth the oracles of God, marvel at them for their beauty and goodness; then, when they discover that our works are not worthy of the words we speak, forthwith they betake themselves to blasphemy, saying it is an idle story and a delusion"(13.3).

And that's precisely what Paul wants to prevent. For that reason we have this strong exhortation to live worthy of the gospel. In the following paragraph Paul will suggest several aspects of what it means to live worthy of the gospel.

I. CONSISTENCY IN CONDUCT (v. 27a)

"Only live your life in a manner worthy of the gospel of Christ." This is the first exhortation of Paul in this letter to the Philippians. So far the apostle has been very personal, telling his readers of his love for them, assuring them of his prayers and testifying to God's grace which sustains the apostle even in prison. Now he turns to the needs of his readers. Although the church didn't seem to have any major problems, Paul knew the power of the Evil One and also the weakness' of Christ's followers. And so he expresses concern that their daily life should be in harmony with their confession.

The first word in our passage is "only"—a word that could be paraphrased as "just one thing" or "now the important thing is this." Paul has just expressed the hope that he will be released and then be able to pay the Philippians a visit. In effect he is now saying: whatever happens to me is not so important; what is really important is that you walk worthy of the gospel.

This is a comprehensive admonition, for it embraces all aspects of daily life. All the exhortations that follow later can be subsumed under this one imperative: walk worthy of the gospel. Paul uses a rather unusual word for "walk" in our passage (*politeuo*—derived from *polis*, meaning city or city-state; the English "politics," "police," etc. are derived from this Greek word). The word means to live as a citizen and to discharge one's duties as a citizen.

From this political meaning of the verb it has been argued that Paul is exhorting the readers to live as good Roman citizens in Philippi and fulfil their civic duties. But that can hardly be Paul's concern in our text. The only other occurrence of this verb in the New Testament is in Acts 23:1, where Luke uses it to describe Paul's way of life in Judaism. In Philippians 3:20 Paul uses the noun *politeuma* (citizenship) to point to that heavenly country to which believers truly belong.

Because Philippi was a "colonia" of Rome, which meant among other things that its citizens were in effect citizens of that city, it was expected of them that they live according to Roman laws and standards. Perhaps, then, Paul chose to use this verb to suggest the Philippian believers must order their lives according to standards of the heavenly Jerusalem, the city of God.

In the Authorized Version of 1611, we read, "Let your conversation be as it becometh the gospel of Christ." This can be easily misconstrued as referring to our speech only, but the word "conversation" had a wider meaning in 1611. It was based on the Latin *conversare*, which means to conduct oneself, to live, to walk. "Walking" is the most common metaphor for the Christian life in the New Testament. It has its roots in the Old Testament. Of Enoch it is said he "walked with God." Abraham is told, "walk before me and be blameless" (Gen. 17:1). And so the Hebrew word *halak* (to walk) becomes the word to describe a person's manner of life, his or her values, standards and goals.

There are several words for "walk" in the Greek New Testament (the most common is *peripateo*—to patter about). In Acts believers are referred to as "the people of the Way." A person's walk is his or her manner of life, and Paul wants the Philippians to live lives that are an honor to the gospel.

The adverb "worthily" (*axios*—our English "axiology," the study of values, is derived from this Greek word) is found repeatedly where the word "walk" is used. In I Thessalonians 2:12 the readers are exhorted to live a life worthy of God, who calls us into his kingdom and glory. In Ephesians 4:1 we are admonished to live worthy of our calling, that is, the call of God heard in the gospel. In Colossians 1:10 we are asked to live worthy of the Lord. Here the call is to walk worthy of the gospel.

The Philippians had heard the gospel from Paul and his associates.

They had shared with Paul in the spread of the gospel (1:5) as well as in its defense (1:7). They are now asked to live in harmony with the content and standards set forth in the gospel. It would be a pity if the Philippians lived in such a manner that the gospel would be despised by non-believers. Christians who have heard the gospel and embraced the good news of redemption must be constantly concerned that this wonderful gospel is not brought into disrepute through their unseemly behavior.

II. FIRMNESS IN FAITH (v. 27b)

"So that, whether I come and see you or am absent and hear about you, I will know that you are standing firm in one spirit, striving side by side with one mind for the faith of the gospel."
    Paul is not absolutely certain about his future. If he should be released, he hopes to visit them, but if not, he hopes to hear about them, and what he wants to hear is that they are standing firm in the face of opposition. The word "to stand" has a literal meaning, but it is also used figuratively for steadfastness, for standing firm. This call to steadfastness is heard in most of Paul's letters; nor is it absent in other apostolic writings. Believers are exhorted to stand firm in the Lord (4:1), firm in the faith (I Cor. 16:13), firm in the freedom Christ has given them (Gal. 5:1). Here they are called upon to stand firm "in one spirit."
    The call to steadfastness suggests that Christians must endure opposition, that they are subject to various kinds of attack, that the Christian life is a warfare. It was a daunting thing to be a follower of Christ in the early centuries of the Christian era, as it still is today in many parts of this world.
    Commentators are divided in their interpretation of the phrase "in one spirit." Some take it to be a reference to the Holy Spirit by which believers are enabled to stand firm. That the Spirit of Christ helps them to stand firm is not in dispute. In fact Paul has already said, even if not in exactly those words, that he looks to the Spirit of Christ to be his helper (1:19). However, the context seems to suggest the "spirit" (*pneuma*) here is a reference to the human spirit and used as a synonym with "one soul." They are to stand firm with inner com-

pactness, they are to be "unanimous" (JB). "Spirit" here is somewhat akin to the French *l'esprit de corps.*

To stand firm, however, does not suggest inactivity or hanging on doggedly. The Philippians are to strive in one soul for the faith of the gospel. The word "strive" appears only here and in 4:3 in the New Testament. It is the word *sunathleo* (literally "playing the game together"; our English "athlete" is derived from this Greek verb). Not all commentators agree that the verb is strictly an athletic figure of speech, since evidently it was also used for struggles in the gladiatorial fights in the arena. Whether we take it to refer to athletic striving or struggles against opponents in warfare or in the arena, the word clearly signifies conflict.

The preposition "sun" conveys the notion of unified striving. They are to contend as if they were one person. To underscore that, Paul adds the phrase "with one soul." The word "soul" has a variety of meanings in the Bible; here it seems to be interchangeable with "spirit" and depicts the unity of purpose in the struggle in which the Philippians were engaged. Of the early believers in Jerusalem it is said they were "one heart and one soul" (Acts 4:32).

The Philippians are exhorted to stand united in their struggle "for the faith of the gospel." It looks as if Paul means the faith which springs from the gospel, rather than their faith in the gospel. The word "faith" is sometimes used as a comprehensive word for the Christian life. It signifies not only what a Christian believes, but also what he or she has experienced through faith in Christ. And this "Christian faith" has its source in the gospel.

To strive for the faith of the gospel would include all the efforts to spread the good news, to grow in grace, to strengthen the life of the church and to preserve the gospel in its integrity.

In the early part of the second century, Ignatius, bishop of Antioch wrote a letter to Polycarp, bishop of Smyrna, both whom lost their lives for the cause of Christ: "Stand firm like an anvil under the hammer. It is like a great athlete to take blows and yet to win the fight." That vocabulary was not forgotten by the church, for in the sixteenth century Theodore Beza reminded the French king of Navarre that "it is truly the lot of the church of God . . . to endure blows and not to strike them. But. . . that it is an anvil which has worn out many hammers."

To stand firm should not be understood as resistance to change. Paul is not encouraging Christians to be stubborn and inflexible. But it certainly includes the notion of steadfastness, something our permissive society abhors. And surely it would also include a warning not to be swayed by every religious wind that happens to be blowing. Dr. Luccock, onetime professor of preaching at Yale, writes in one of his sermons that many Christians are like the invalids at the pool of Bethesda, constantly waiting for the water to bubble, and then they step in. The last thing we as twentieth-century Christians should engage in is "bubble chasing."

III. FEARLESS ATTITUDE (v. 28)

"And are in no way intimidated by your opponents. For them this is evidence of their destruction, but of your salvation. And this is God's doing." Having encouraged his readers to stand firm, Paul now counsels them not to be intimidated by their opponents. The verb "intimidated" is rarely used in the Greek Bible. In classical times it was used to describe horses that had become frightened and skittish. The Philippians are not to run away scared like startled horses, one might say. If they stand together in unity this potential danger would be minimized.

Who their opponents were is not spelled out. Some think Paul is anticipating chapter 3, where the opponents of the gospel are those Jewish-Christian preachers who were introducing legalism into the gospel. However, here it seems rather obvious that Paul has non-Christians in mind, for he speaks of their destruction. If the enemies mentioned in chapter 3 should be non-Christian Jews, then Paul may in fact have the same opponents in mind. It looks as if these enemies of the gospel were threatening the Philippians with persecution, and Paul wants them to face these opponents fearlessly.

The fearless attitude of Christians in the face of suffering often impressed onlookers in the early centuries and sometimes became the occasion for enemies of the Christian faith to embrace the gospel. Fearlessness characterizes the victor—the student who sits for an exam with confidence, for he knows the material; the warrior who faces the enemy, for he knows the outcome is certain to be victory; the athlete who through long experience knows the prize is within his grasp.

Fearlessness is evidence that the believer is on the way to salvation, whereas for the opponents it is a sign of their demise. To be undaunted in the face of opposition signifies that believers are sure of ultimate victory. Whether the enemies of the gospel see in the steadfastness of the Christians a sign that they themselves are on the losing side is not certain. What is certain is when the followers of Christ endure suffering for their faith with patient endurance, they can be sure God will ultimately deliver them and bring them into his eternal kingdom, whereas those who persecute God's people have only the grim prospect of destruction and ruin in the sense of eternal perdition.

The closing words of v. 28, "and this from God," probably applies to all of the preceding paragraph, rather than just to "salvation" and "perdition." God alone gives his children the strength to walk worthy of the gospel, to stand united against the onslaughts of the enemy, and he, too, assures his followers of eternal life and threatens his enemies with eternal doom.

IV. COURAGE IN SUFFERING (vv. 29,30)

"For he has graciously granted you the privilege not only of believing in Christ, but of suffering for him as well—since you are having the same struggle that you saw I had and now hear that I still have."

Suffering has attended the lives of believers all through the centuries. What surprises us is that Paul looks upon suffering as a privilege. It is a gift given to believers as evidence of God's grace. The word "to give" (*charizomai*) means to give graciously or freely as a favor. The passive voice of the verb signifies it is God who has so privileged them. Of course, Paul is not speaking of suffering in general, the kind that all humankind is subject to, but specifically he has suffering for the sake of Christ in mind. "For Christ" can mean simply that the Philippians suffered because they belonged to Christ. It can mean also "for the sake of Christ" because of their love and devotion to Christ. It is even possible to render the phrase as "in place of

Christ." This would then be in line with Colossians 1:24,25, where Paul expresses the wish to fill up what is lacking in Christ's suffering. Not that the sufferings of Christians can atone for the sins of others, as did Christ's sufferings and his death, but believers can suffer on behalf of others in the hope they might come to Christ.

Not only suffering but believing too is a gracious gift of God. The verb "believe" is in the present tense, connoting an ongoing relationship of trust in Christ.

To encourage the Philippians in their suffering, Paul links their sufferings with his own. "You are now engaged in the same conflict." They and Paul are sharing in the same *agon* (from which we derive our word "agony"). It is a word that comes from the racetrack but eventually came to signify any conflict, struggle or battle. Here it refers to the untiring toil and labor in spreading the gospel, with the added thought of opposition to the gospel often leading to physical suffering. *Agon* is wide enough in meaning to embrace both the inner agonies and the physical harassment early Christians had to endure as they sought to spread the gospel in the first decades of the Christian era. Since the Philippians shared in the spread of the gospel (1:5) from the time the church was established, they also had to endure the sufferings from their opponents, as did Paul himself.

The Philippians were of course aware of the sufferings Paul had to endure for the sake of the gospel. They had "seen" him suffer when the church was founded, when he was beaten and thrown into jail. And now they "heard" he was in prison again for the sake of the gospel. The readers then are in good company, and they can take courage from the fact that, to use the words of Peter, "the same kinds of suffering are going over their brothers (and sisters) in all the world" (I Pet. 5:9).

As Christians living in countries where religious freedom is guaranteed, we know relatively little of suffering for Christ's sake. But our gospel is an offense to our godless society, and opposition to the Christian faith breaks out very quickly. Christians have not always suffered in every part of the world, but somewhere at any given time the church is being harassed. So, while we thank God for holding his hand over us for the moment, we must never forget that the saints enter into the eternal kingdom through much tribulation.

Review Questions

1. *Name some practical dimensions of walking "worthy of the gospel" in our society today.*

2. *What does "unity in the spirit" mean in the practical sense?*

3. *Does striving for the faith of the gospel mean we must constantly defend the gospel?*

4. *How would you distinguish between standing firm in the faith and just plain stubbornness?*

5. *What form does "suffering for Christ" take occasionally even in our free society?*

6. *How should we relate to our fellow Christians in other parts of the world where believers are suffering for the faith?*

CHAPTER SIX

Unity through Humility (2:1-11)

If then there is any encouragement in Christ, any consolation from love, any sharing in the Spirit, any compassion and sympathy, make my joy complete: be of the same mind, having the same love, being in full accord and of one mind. Do nothing from selfish ambition or conceit, but in humility regard others as better than yourselves. Let each of you look not to your own interests, but to the interests of others. Let the same mind be in you that was in Christ Jesus, who, though he was in the form of God, did not regard equality with God as something to be exploited, but emptied himself, taking the form of a slave, being born in human likeness. And being found in human form, he humbled himself and became obedient to the point of death - even death on a cross. Therefore God also highly exalted him and gave him the name that is above every name, so that at the name of Jesus every knee should bend, in heaven and on earth and under the earth, and every tongue should confess that Jesus Christ is Lord, to the glory of God the Father (Phiippians 2:1-11).

It was the hope of our Lord that some day there would be one flock and one shepherd (John. 10:16). And his prayer for his followers, as he stood in the shadow of the cross, was that they all might be one (Jn. 17:11). The early church was threatened again and again by dissension and division. There were cultural barriers to overcome. One might mention the tension between the Hellenists and the Hebraists within the Jewish community (see Acts 6). More serious was the need to break down barriers between Jews and Samaritans, Jews and Gentiles.

The early church fought valiantly to prevent ethnic, social and economic differences in the church from destroying the unity of the body of Christ. We are not certain whether the church at Philippi was threatened by divisions within its ranks. Paul's appeal to stand united is probably an attempt to prevent fighting between members of the church from breaking out. Paul does single out two women (4:2), who evidently were not getting along with each other, and asks them to be of one mind.

In the paragraph that lies before us Paul appeals to the Philippians to be in full accord with each other. The greatest threat to unity seems to be human pride and selfishness. And so Paul will give a brief portrait of our Lord who humbled himself to the point of dying for others in order to bring humankind back to God. If the readers will have the mind of Christ (v. 5), unity will not be hard to maintain. Let us look first at the spiritual underpinnings for unity in the church.

I. THE SPIRITUAL UNDERPINNINGS (v. 1)

A. Encouragement in Christ
"If then there is encouragement in Christ." We have a series of true to fact conditional clauses beginning with "if," and for that reason the "if" should be rendered as "since." Paul has no doubts that there is, in fact, encouragement in Christ. It is a given.

"Encouragement" is translated from the Greek *paraklesis* which has other meanings as well, such as comfort, consolation, exhortation and encouragement. It is not quite clear whether it is Christ who encourages the readers or whether it is Paul, who is in fellowship with Christ, and who encourages them to strive for unity. Perhaps it is both.

B. Consolation of Love

The word *paramuthion* can also be rendered as comfort and encouragement, and so it is hard to make a clear distinction between these two words. Basically the word means to speak to someone in a friendly way. There is consolation that comes from the mutual love that Christians have for each other. To know that Paul loved the Philippians would also be a source of comfort and consolation. However, the reference is probably to the love of Christ. The deep assurance that Christ has loved us gives great comfort to the believers, especially in times of trials and sufferings.

C. Fellowship of the Spirit

The word *koinonia* means basically to share, to have in common. The word occurs six times in this letter (1:5,7; 2:1; 3:10; 4:14,15). It is usually translated as "fellowship." The question now is, did the Spirit bring them into fellowship with each other, or does Paul mean all the Philippians share and participate in the same Spirit? Another possibility is that Paul has a "spiritual" fellowship in mind. Perhaps these meanings are not mutually exclusive.

There is some dispute about the meaning of "spirit" (*pneuma*). Does Paul mean the Holy Spirit? If we are to take 2 Corinthians 13:13 as a parallel, then the matter is clear, for there Paul speaks of the "fellowship of the Holy Spirit." Also, we are told that by one Spirit (i.e. the Holy Spirit) we are all baptized into one body (I Cor. 12:13). Assuming the Spirit of God is meant, we might say the Spirit creates the fellowship of the saints (subj. gen.), but the saints also participate in the same Spirit (obj. gen.).

D. Compassion and Sympathy

These two words are so similar in meaning one could render them as sympathy and compassion instead of compassion and sympathy. The first noun (*splagchna*) occurred in 1:8, where it expressed Paul's affection for his readers. Here the word points to the compassion of Christ which the readers experienced when they became Christians.

That would also be the case with the *oiktrimos*, meaning the pity, the mercy, the sympathy of Christ for the Philippians. We should, however, not rule out the possibility that Paul has in mind the compassion and sympathy which believers show each other. Those who have experienced the mercies of God, want to show mercy to others too. And that provides a good foundation for the fostering of unity in the church.

Assuming that these spiritual graces are found in the church, Paul now makes his appeal.

II. THE APOSTOLIC APPEAL (v. 2)

"Make my joy complete: be of the same mind, having the same love, being in full accord and of one mind." There was much in the Philippian church that gave Paul cause to rejoice, but now he asks his readers to fill his cup of joy to the brim. Although at first blush the exhortation may appear to be selfish, it is the readers the apostle is concerned about. Where there is a good relationship between parent and child, teacher and student, pastor and church, an appeal to make the parent, teacher or pastor happy can carry great weight.

Paul wants them to "think the same thing." Surely he is not encouraging a drab uniformity. He does not expect everyone to have the same opinion on every subject. But he wants them to live harmoniously with each other. And when there is a harmony of attitudes, differences of opinion do not easily drive people apart. (When it comes to the matter of false teaching, of course, we have a different situation.)

The apostle wants the Philippians to have the same love. The love he has in mind is no doubt the love of God shed abroad in their hearts by the Holy Spirit. The word "same" may suggest that Paul does not want anyone to lag behind in showing love to others. God's love, manifested in Christ, is an outgoing love; it reaches to the lost and the lowly. And that is the kind of love Paul wants his readers to demonstrate in their life together.

To underscore his appeal, the apostle seems to pile up synonyms. Someone has called this verse the tautology of earnestness. He wants them to be "onesouled" (*sumpsuchoi*), harmonious, united in spirit. This compound appears only here in the New Testament.

Finally, they are to "have one mind." Again this should not be understood as ruling out a variety of viewpoints which people may express in friendly discussion and debate. Life would be very dull without such give-and-take. But believers are to have the same purpose in life. The goal of a Christian community is to live in harmony. And Paul expresses his appeal in a fourfold way, hoping the Philippians will get the point.

When the members of a church are cut more or less from the same cloth ethnically, socially and historically, it may be easier to maintain unity. Although, human nature being what it is, even in such cases tensions arise easily. When the members of a congregation come from different backgrounds, bridge building takes on even greater significance. But if a church is to grow and fulfil its mission, there must be harmony. Paul now mentions several graces that contribute to this spirit of harmony.

III . THE NECESSARY GRACES (vv. 3,4)

"Do nothing from selfish ambition or conceit, but in humility regard others as better than yourselves. Let each of you look not to your own interests, but to the interests of others." The apostle mentions two forces that are destructive to unity, namely conceit and selfishness. To counter these evils, two Christian graces are recommended: humility and concern for others.

A. Humility

One of the ethical dangers threatening the unity of the Philippian church was "selfish ambition" *(eritheia)*. We encountered this word in 1:17, where it denoted the rival preaching of Paul's opponents. Here too it refers to selfish ambition which leads to rivalries and factions which drive people apart.

The other danger mentioned is "conceit" *(kenodoxia)*. Although a cognate noun is found in Galatians 5:26, this is the only place in the New Testament where this compound is found. Literally the word means "empty glory." It is the cheap desire to boast which springs from pride. C.H. Spurgeon compared such people with empty wagons, which always rattle more loudly than full ones.

How are such evils to be overcome? By humility *(tapeinophrosune)*. Literally the word means to "think lowly," and in profane Greek it is usually used in a derogatory sense of servility or shameful lowliness. But in the New Testament there is nothing grovelling about this word. It has been cleansed and elevated by our Lord, who was meek and lowly in heart (Mt. 11:29).

Humility has nothing to do with the feeling of worthlessness, the feeling of shame and inferiority which so often burdens God's children. People who know they have been created by God and redeemed at great cost should have a healthy self-respect. There is no suggestion here that Christians should put on a mask of humility by the way they walk or dress or put themselves down.

Humility expresses itself not in self-disparagement, but in treating others with respect. To regard others better than ourselves is not an encouragement to hypocrisy when, for example, we know we do some things better than others. In the presence of God we all stand on one footing, and so even when others have a more lowly position or are more limited in some respects than we are, we can still treat them with respect and appreciation as fellow members of the body of Christ.

B. Concern for Others

"Let each of you look not to your own interests, but to the interests of others." There are, of course, legitimate self-interests. "For all must carry their own loads" (Gal. 6:5). There are certain things that no one can do for us. Here, however, Paul warns against selfishness. The verb "to look" (*skopeo*) means to look at attentively, to fix one's attention on something with deep interest. In 2:21 the writer complains that all others (apart from Timothy) are seeking their own interests. A distinguishing mark of love is that it does not seek its own (I Cor. 13:5). Of Christ it is said he did not please himself (Rom. 15:3).

It has been suggested that Paul was encouraging his readers to look at the good points of others and find in them an incentive to emulate these. Another way of reading the text is Christians should not be so occupied with their own spiritual attainments that they fail to see what is exemplary in the lives of others. As practical applications of our text, one might let such interpretations stand, but they do not seem to get to the heart of what Paul is saying here.

To overcome selfishness the Philippians are to look also at the interests of others. The word "also" is missing in some manuscripts but is well attested. The "also" offers the contrast, for no one can live without paying attention to his or her bodily and other needs. But we are to love our neighbors as ourselves and not be preoccupied with ourselves.

True humility and concern for others was modelled supremely by our Lord, and so Paul will now hold up the example of Christ to motivate the readers in the practice of these Christian graces which make for unity in the church.

IV. THE CHRISTOLOGICAL MOTIVATION (vv. 5-11)

"Let the same mind be in you that was in Christ Jesus" (v. 5). This exhortation introduces the Christological hymn that follows. Believers are encouraged to adopt an attitude towards each other as Christ had.

Not all scholars agree that the following verses are an early Christian hymn. Ernst Lohmeyer thinks it is a eucharistic hymn, originally in Aramaic and then translated into Greek. This is hard to prove. The verses do seem to have a strophic arrangement and so we should at least acknowledge that the verses have a hymnic structure. Verses 6 to 8 describe Christ's humiliation, and then, verses 9 to 11 speak of his exaltation. Since there are some unusual words in this passage, some scholars hold that Paul borrowed this hymn from another source. There would be nothing wrong with that, but we should not think that Paul was incapable of composing such solemn and stately lines.

A. Christ's Humiliation (vv. 6-8)
1. His Condescension (v. 6). "Who, though he was in the form of God, did not regard equality with God as something to be exploited." The English word "condescension" today is in bad taste, suggesting a patronizing attitude. However, I am using it in its original sense of lowering oneself to the level of an inferior. The passage begins with the assertion that Christ, who existed in the form of God, did not regard his equality with God as something to be used for his

own advantage. To be in the form of God means Christ was and is divine. He was divine by nature. He shared in God's majesty and glory.

But he did not exploit this exalted position for selfish ends. We have a most unusual word here and it has been understood in different ways. *Harpagmos* occurs only here in the Greek Bible and is derived from the verb *harpazo*, meaning to snatch or to seize. One might say then that Christ did not think equality with God was something to be seized. The King James Version says: "He did not think it robbery to be equal with God." But if he already possessed equality with God, why would he want to, or not want to, seize it? Another way of reading it is Christ did not treat his equality with God as a prize, a treasure to be greedily clutched. On the contrary, he resigned the glories of heaven and came to us here on earth. He did not cling to equality with God. A third way of interpreting this verse is he did not use his privileged position to his own advantage. He did not exploit his exalted position selfishly. Perhaps there is an allusion here to the first Adam who thought being like God could be grasped. He tried but failed miserably. Jesus, by contrast, was like God, but he gave up all the advantages and privileges of such an exalted state and lowered himself to our level in order to bring us back to God.

2. His Abnegation (v. 7a). "He emptied himself." This metaphor suggests that Christ gave up all he had. If one tries to be more precise in defining what it was he "emptied himself" of, one usually runs into difficulties. That he left the glory of heaven behind when he came to earth is clear. But when it is suggested he gave up some attributes of deity when he became man, one is hard pressed to say which ones.

The verb "to empty" *(kenoo)* should be understood metaphorically (not metaphysically), meaning Christ poured out himself, putting himself totally at the disposal of people. He became poor so we might become rich through his poverty .

3. His Subordination (v. 7b). "Taking on the form of a slave." This seems to be a commentary on the self-emptying just mentioned. Again we have the noun "form" *(morphe)* which was used in verse 6, where it was said Christ was in the form of God. To be in the form of God means to partake of the nature of deity; to be in the form of a slave then means to adopt the nature and character of a slave.

Although some interpreters take the word "slave" to be reminiscent of the servant of Yahweh in Isaiah 53 who suffers and dies for others, it is probably simply a reference to the practice of slavery in Paul's day. It means then that Christ, like a slave, was deprived of all his rights and privileges. A particularly telling example of what it meant to take on the form of a slave was the washing of his disciples' feet (Jn. 13:3-5).

4. His Identification (v. 7c). "Being born in human likeness." Christ identified himself with the human race; he became in all respects like other human beings. That he was without sin did not make him less human. He was "found in human form." A different word is used for "form" (*schema*) at this point. In the early Christian centuries there were the so-called Docetists who held that although Jesus looked like a man and he appeared like other human beings, he really was not truly human. But that was a misunderstanding.

Jesus was conceived and born of a human mother (Gal. 4:4). Although he did not have a human father, John insists that anyone who denies that Jesus came in the flesh is Antichrist (I John 4:3). To be "found" in the form of a man is probably a Semitism, meaning "he was."

Perhaps one could illustrate the difference between *morphe* (form) and *schema* (form) in this way: a baby, a child, a boy, a youth and an old man all have the *morphe* of a human male, but the *schema* (appearance) varies. Or, roses, daffodils, tulips and primroses all partake of the *morphe* of a flower, but the outward *schema* varies. So Christ partook of the very nature of God, but when he was born he took on the likeness of a human being.

To say that Christ is truly human, does not mean he was merely a man. He always remained fully divine. Unfortunately his contemporaries by and large failed to see him as the son of God.

5. His Humiliation (v. 8a). "He humbled himself and became obedient." When it is said he "emptied" himself, we think of Christ's incarnation. When it is added he "humbled" himself, we think of Christ's life here on earth. From the cradle to the grave he humbled himself. The active voice of the verb suggests this was a voluntary decision on his part.

Christ did not strive for power, for his rights or for a high position in society. He was not out to make a name for himself. He deliberately became obedient to his Father's will. His food was to do the will of the Father and to complete his work (Jn 4:34). His obedience to the Father in the end took him to Gethsemane where in the face of death he humbly confessed, "Not my will but yours be done."

6. His Crucifixion (v. 8b). "He became obedient to the point of death—even death on a cross." At the cross Christ's obedience, as well as his humiliation, reached its nadir. By the standards of the first century, no experience was so loathsomely degrading as crucifixion. Today the cross is venerated as a sacred symbol; it is even worn as jewellery, and so it is hard for us to imagine the horror and disgust the mention of the cross would have provoked.

For Roman readers the cross meant Christ was a criminal; for the Jews to hang upon a tree meant Christ was under a divine curse (Deut. 21:23). But the word "cross," which was an obscenity in Paul's day, came to symbolize the supreme sacrifice of Christ for the sins of the world, assuring us of eternal redemption.

B. Christ's Exaltation (vv. 9-11)

The story of Jesus did not end with the cross. If it had, we would have had no gospel, no church, no New Testament, no Lord's day. We would still be in our sins and without hope. In the paragraph on Christ's humiliation Paul makes our Lord the chief actor. But when he turns to his exaltation, God takes over, as it were. Christ humbled himself and the Father exalted him. The exaltation of Christ was the Father's "Amen" to the Son's "It is finished."

1. The Affirmation (v. 9). "Therefore God also highly exalted him and gave him the name that is above every name." An inferential conjunction *dio* (therefore) marks the transition from the depths of shame, the cross, to the heights of glory. God vindicated and approved of his Son's humiliation by exalting him highly . Jesus' words, "whoever humbles himself will be exalted" (Mt. 23:12), were fulfilled in his own experience.

In speaking of Christ's exaltation by the Father Paul uses a compound verb—*huperupsoo*, one of the many *huper* (over) compounds found in Paul's letters. God has lifted up his Son to the highest possible position. The exaltation is not described in stages as was Christ's humiliation. One verb declares that Christ was raised from the lowest depths to the highest heights. "And he gave him a name that is above every name." This is another way of saying God highly exalted Christ; it amplifies and interprets the exaltation. In Paul's day a person's name not only distinguished him or her from others, but it revealed a person's character and personality. God graciously (*charizomai*) gave Jesus Christ a name that is above all other names. He gave him his own name Kurios (Lord).

For a Jew there was nothing higher than the superlative name Yahweh. This Hebrew name was rendered *kurios* in the Greek Septuagint. In Isaiah 42:8 Yahweh claims, "I am the Lord, that is my name." It is his and no one else's. But he gave this name to Jesus after Christ had completed his work on earth. This means Jesus now exercises universal lordship. All authority is given to him in heaven and on earth (Mt. 28:18).

2. The purpose (vv. 10,11). Grammatically these two verses express the purpose of God in exalting his Son. One purpose is expressed in verse 10: "So that at the name of Jesus every knee should bend, in heaven and on earth and under the earth." Sometimes purpose and result run together, and that may be the case in our text. When it is said every knee shall bend at the name of Jesus, Paul is reminding his readers that the one who has received a name above every other name, and who is now universal Lord is none other than the historical Jesus of Nazareth—the Jesus who humbled himself and died on the cross for the sins of the world.

What is said of God in Isaiah 45:23, "Unto me every knee shall bow, every tongue shall swear allegiance," is said here of the exalted Christ. In honor of Jesus (i.e., Jesus' name) every knee shall bow. To bend the knee is a common oriental gesture for paying homage. And while this kind of homage is given to Jesus in the church, Paul casts the net more widely here: he anticipates universal acknowledgement of the lordship of Christ.

Heaven, earth and under the earth are three adjectives in Greek which function here as nouns and speak of creation in its totality. In Paul's day people spoke of a three-storied universe and so universality was expressed in this threefold manner. Although the grammar allows us to read these words as either neuter or masculine, the context suggests we are dealing with animate things—people, angels and perhaps even demons. This is not universalism in the sense that everyone will be saved in the end, but speaks rather of universal submission and acknowledgement in the end, that Jesus is Lord.

To express this in another way: "And every tongue should confess that Jesus Christ is Lord, to the glory of God the Father" (v. 11). This verse speaks of the goal or the consequence of Christ's humiliation and his exaltation to the Father's right hand. To bend the knee and confess with the mouth are parallel ways of speaking of submission to the lordship of Christ.

The affirmation that Jesus Christ is Lord was probably the earliest Christian confessional formula, at least in Gentile churches. Those who confessed Christ as Lord had the assurance they would be saved (Rom. 10:9,10). It is only with the help of the Holy Spirit that people can make this confession (I Cor. 12:3). As it turned out, this confession of Christ's lordship, brought early Christians into a head-on collision with a totalitarian state that demanded absolute loyalty from its subjects.

To confess Christ as Lord does not mean that in the end all living beings will make a personal confession of faith in Christ, but it means that in the end Christ will be acknowledged as Lord by every creature. The proclamation that Jesus is Lord springs from glad hearts in the case of Christ's followers. Those who reject Christ will, however, in the end also have to acknowledge that he is Lord and surrender to him.

And when that happens God will not be embarrassed, for such universal acknowledgement of Christ's lordship is "to the glory of God the Father." These climactic words are to be linked not simply with the "confession" of Christ's lordship, but to the lordship of Christ himself. Jesus has not only the title "Lord" but also the prerogatives of lordship. But his lordship is not a threat to God, for the purpose of Christ's exaltation is that God should be all in all (I Cor. 15:28).

Although we do not yet see all principalities and powers in submission to Christ, those who have responded to the gospel confess Christ as Lord over their lives. They belong to him with all their dreams and goals, their possessions and their gifts, for "whether we live or die we are the Lord's" (Rom. 14:8).

Review Questions

1. *Name some of the common factors that tend to create disunity in the church.*

2. *Is it possible to be loyal to one's own denomination without falling into the trap of denominationalism?*

3. *How might Paul's exhortation to "regard others as better than ourselves" express itself in daily life?*

4. *From this passage show how Christian ethics find their supreme motivation in the example of Christ.*

5. *If Christ's self-humiliation is a model for us, how might this express itself? How might believers in a "high position" manifest Christ's spirit in this regard?*

6. *In the practical sense what does it mean for us to confess that Jesus is our Lord?*

CHAPTER SEVEN

Working Out Our Salvation (2:12-18)

Therefore, my beloved, just as you have always obeyed me, not only in my presence, but much more now in my absence, work our your own salvation with fear and trembling; for it is God who is at work in you, enabling you both to will and to work for his good pleasure. Do all things without murmuring and arguing, so that you may be blameless and innocent, children of God without blemish in the midst of a crooked and perverse generation, in which you shine like stars in the world. It is by your holding fast to the word of life that I can boast on the day of Christ that I did not run in vain or labor in vain. But even if I am being poured out as a libation over the sacrifice and the offering of your faith, I am glad and rejoice with all of you - and in the same way you also must be glad and rejoice with me (Philippians 2:12-18).

The hortatory section which began in 1:27 is continued in the paragraph that lies before us. The passage has many facets and makes it hard to decide on a theme that will embrace the different emphases of our text. I have chosen the topic from the second part of verse 12, "Work out your own salvation with fear and trembling," and shall try to relate the teachings of this paragraph to this theme.

It is not easy to say precisely what Paul means when he exhorts his readers (and us) to "work out" (*katergazomai*) their own salvation. Although the verb "to work" is used twenty times by Paul, nowhere else is "salvation" the object of this verb. The verb means to bring about, to produce, to create.

Proceeding from the English, some readers have understood "working out" to mean we should let others know about our salvation. "Work out" what God has "worked in," as I have heard it said. Paul does want his readers to witness to their faith (v. 15), but that is hardly the meaning of this exhortation.

Some scholars have taken the word "salvation" in a sociological rather than a theological sense to describe the spiritual health of the community. In other words, Paul is urging his readers to do whatever they can to make sure the congregation is spiritually healthy. That Paul wants the members of the church to be concerned about the spiritual welfare of the body of Christ goes without saying. Such an interpretation does make this exhortation easier to understand, but one wonders whether it is not too easy.

I would suggest that Paul is speaking of personal salvation. *Soteria* (salvation) means more than corporate well-being. Also, Paul asks the Philippians to work out "their own" salvation. This does not mean we can save ourselves. Salvation is from beginning to end a gift of God's grace. However, we are individually responsible to manifest the grace of God which we have experienced. To pursue holiness, to be filled with the Spirit, to make our calling and election sure, are other ways of saying what it means to work out our salvation.

That it should be done with "fear and trembling" does not mean we live in fear of losing our salvation, but it speaks of reverence, awe and humility in the presence of God. It is not a slavish fear but rather it is an idiomatic expression to underscore that working out our salvation is serious business.

Let us now turn to the beginning of our passage and ask ourselves first how working out our salvation might express itself.

I. THE PRACTICAL EXPRESSION (v. 12)

"Therefore, my beloved, just as you have always obeyed me, not only in my presence, but much more now in my absence, work out your salvation with fear and trembling." The passage begins with an inferential conjunction ("so then") which means it is related in some way to the previous pericope. Very likely it is Christ's obedience which led him to the cross that Paul has in mind when he exhorts his readers to be obedient to the teachings of the apostle. He commends them for having obeyed in the past, and encourages them to work out their salvation by being obedient in the future.

The apostle addresses his readers very affectionately at this point ("my beloved"). This form of address is often found when Paul makes earnest appeals (I Cor. 10:14; 15:58; 2 Cor. 7:1; 12:19; Phil. 3:1). Although the word "beloved" (*agapetoi*) is used also to convey the truth that believers are objects of God's love, here the pronoun "my" makes clear it is Paul who wants them to feel the warmth of his affection for them.

Before exhorting them to work out their salvation, Paul commends them for their obedience in the past. He does not say whether they were obedient to God or to the apostles, but that is not really necessary, for to respond positively to the gospel and to the apostolic teachings would also be obedience rendered to God. Very likely the initial response of the Philippians to the message of the gospel is included in this reference to past obedience. But since they began the Christian life, they had been obedient to the teachings of the apostles. This was in line with the spirit of Jesus, who became obedient to the point of death (v. 8).

Paul, however, wants this life of obedience, by which the readers work out their salvation, to be lived regardless of his personal presence. The force of his personal or bodily presence should not be necessary for them to continue to walk the Christian way. The fall of humans into sin was brought about by disobedience and so redemption is obtained by the obedience of Christ. We should then not be surprised to find the Christian life described as a life of obedience. To believe the gospel is to obey it. Paul speaks of the "obedience of faith" (Rom. 15:18). Dietrich Bonhoeffer was not far off the mark when he said "without obedience our faith is pious humbug."

But we ask: where do we get the strength to do the will of the Father, to obey the commandments of our Lord, to hold to the apostolic teachings, to work out our salvation? The answer is given in verse 13.

II. THE DIVINE STRENGTH (v. 13)

"For it is God who is at work in you, enabling you both to will and to work for his good pleasure." Although the apostolic exhortation is somewhat overwhelming, the believer is not left to his or her own resources. God is working powerfully within each of them. He not only began the good work (1:6) but he keeps on working in them. As it often is in the New Testament the imperative of the previous verse (v. 12) is supported by the indicative of verse 13. God supplies what he demands.

Paul has been charged with inconsistency because in verse 12 it almost appears as if we are responsible for our salvation, and in verse 13 he makes it clear that all is of God. Some have seen the "monergism" (God does it alone) of verse 13 as contradicting the "synergism" (we work together with God) of verse 12. But God's work of grace in the lives of his people is always related to the human response, our openness, our obedience. And so when Paul stresses human responsibility at one point and sovereign grace at another, we should not accuse him of inconsistency. There is simply more than one side to the question.

The verb *energeo* (to work) is used almost exclusively by Paul in the New Testament and it carries the notion of a supernatural power working (it also can be used for the supernatural working of Satan; 2 Thess. 2:9). The phrase "in you" could also be rendered as "among you." However, it may not be necessary to decide whether we should read this in a collective or in an individual sense, since both are true. In order to work in the Christian community, God must work in the individual.

And not only does God work in the believer to make him or her willing to obey God, but he also supplies the power to carry out such resolve. "To will" and "to do" are both in the present tense, suggesting this is something that must go on throughout the believer's life. But what does the prepositional phrase "in behalf of his good pleasure" mean? The pronoun "his" is not in the original text and for that reason some scholars think the noun *eudokia* (good pleasure) speaks of the goodwill of the believer to do what pleases God. That the noun can refer to human goodwill is clear from 1:15. However, the arguments in favor of understanding *eudokia* as God's goodwill, are more compelling. The omission of the pronoun "his" does not rule out this meaning . The purpose of God's ongoing work in the hearts and lives of his children is his good pleasure. And he is pleased to see the good work which he began in us completed on the day of Christ (1:6). Our salvation, which we are asked to "work out," is his pleasure.

When we stand before God on the last day, we will not take credit for having worked out our salvation, for we will see more clearly then that had it not been for God's constant work in us by his Spirit, our experience of salvation would have been truncated. We are saved by grace, not by works. However, works are the evidence of God's grace in our lives.

III. THE CONSTANT DANGER (vv. 14,15a)

"Do all things without murmuring and arguing, so that you may be blameless and innocent, children of God without blemish in the midst of a crooked and perverse generation." In the process of working out their salvation, believers need to be on guard against all those things which endanger spiritual progress. One of these is the temptation to grumble. The Greek word *gongusmos* is an onomatopoeic word, in which the sound and the sense agree, as in the English word "murmur." The word *dialogismos* (from which we derive "dialogue") covers a wide area of meaning, but basically it means argument or dispute.

Paul's language reminds us of Old Testament descriptions of Israel in the days of Moses, when the people grumbled and complained about their lot as they made their way through the wilderness to the promised land (Num. 11:1-6; 14:1-4; 20:2; 21:4,5). Since the complaints of Israel in the wilderness were frequently aimed at God, some readers have suggested that Paul also has dissatisfaction with God in mind when he warned the Philippians against grumbling and disputing, murmuring and questioning—which are forms of rebellion against God.

However, it is also recorded that ancient Israel rebelled against Moses who led them out of Egypt through the wilderness. And so it may be that Paul has the complaining and disputing among the members of the church in mind. Since Paul has already exhorted the readers to unity (2:1ff.) this would be another appeal to quit sniping at each other. In the other three occurrences of the word "grumble" (Acts 6:1; 1 Pet. 4:9; Jn. 7:12) the context favors dissatisfied grumblings against other people. In our text we have a plural and this could include all the complaints about other church members, church leaders and perhaps even unbelievers at whose hands Christians were often humiliated. If the complaining and disputing which Paul has in mind is directed at people, then by implication it is also directed at God. There is a saying in the Didache (3:6) that is a parallel to Paul's exhortation here: "My child, do not be a grumbler, for grumbling leads to blasphemy. "

There is a profound reason why Paul exhorts his readers not to rebel against God and complain about others. It is expressed in a purpose clause: "in order that you might be blameless and innocent, children of God without blemish." The adjective "blameless" (*amemptos*) is derived from a verb that means to find fault with, and here it means to be without blame, reproach or fault (cf. Lk. 1:6; Phil. 3:6; 1 Thess. 2:11; 3:13).

The word innocent (*akeraios*) is akin to a verb that means to mix or mingle. Here it means unmixed, pure and sincere. The two adjectives taken together suggest the readers were to live in such a way that no one could accuse them of bad conduct. The verb "become" indicates that we never attain to complete perfection but that we are always on the way. To render the verb as "prove yourselves to be" in the sense of demonstrating that they were in fact blameless does not seem to be the best way of rendering the verb "to become." The suggestion that Paul is looking forward to the *parousia* and wants his readers to be without blame when that great day comes is otherwise appropriate, and Paul does express this hope repeatedly. However, in our passage he wants the Philippians to be without blame and reproach in the midst of the present corrupt and sinful world.

They are to be "children of God without blemish." This addition seems to be in apposition to what has just been stated. They are already God's children, and now they must demonstrate by their behavior that they belong to God's family and reflect God's character. In the words of Jesus, they are to "become sons of your Father who is in heaven" (Mt. 5:45).

The word "unblemished" is frequently found in the Old Testament (LXX) to describe sacrificial animals which were to have no physical defects (Ex. 29:1). But it was also used of the godly person, and that is how it is used in the New Testament. The purpose of our election, says Paul, is to be holy and "without blemish" (Eph. 1:4). It is Paul's hope that in the end he will be able to present to Christ a bride, the church, without blemish (Eph. 5:27).

Believers are to live sincere, innocent, blameless lives, like true children of God "in the midst of a crooked and perverse generation." These words are used in the Old Testament to describe the generation of Israelites who came out of Egypt (Dt. 32:5). The Philippians are not to be like that wilderness generation. Incidentally, it should be noted that Paul sees the church as the replacement of rebellious Israel. The church stands in continuity, however, with that faithful remnant within the nation of Israel that remained true to Yahweh.

Whereas the words "crooked and perverse" characterize the rebellious Israel of Moses' generation, in our text they apply to the unbelieving world as a whole. The Philippians have to live in the midst of a society that is "crooked" and "twisted"—a world that is under the judgement of God.

Not only do believers have to live in the midst of a world that is morally corrupt; they also have a mission to perform in the society in which God has placed them. It should be noted that Paul does not encourage fleeing the world or a ghetto mentality. Christians are to be "in" the world but not "of" the world, as Jesus said. If the church tried to remove itself physically and geographically from the unbelieving world, it could not carry out its mission. What its mission is will now be stated. Mission is the concrete evidence that we are working out our salvation.

IV. THE CONCRETE EVIDENCE (vv. 15b,16)

"In which you shine like stars in the world. It is by your holding fast to the word of life that I can boast on the day of Christ that I did not run in vain or labor in vain." In a society that is hostile to the Christian faith, believers are to shine as lights. "You are the light of the world," said Jesus to his followers (Mt 5:14). The voice of the verb "to shine" is either passive or middle. When read as passive it means to become visible, to appear, to be seen. If, however, it is read as a middle voice, it means to shine, to flash, to sparkle.

The word "light" (*phoster*)—found only here and in Revelation 21:11 is a light-giving body, a luminary, a beacon. The believers in that case are said to be lights shining in the world of humanity, which is thought of as living in darkness. However, since *phosteres* is used in the LXX to denote the heavenly bodies such as stars created on the fourth day (Gen. 1:14,16), it would be perfectly legitimate to render the word as "stars." In that case, the believers are described as stars shining in the sky, lighting up the darkness of the world.

Light and darkness are not to be understood as categories of physics; they are moral concepts in the Scriptures. Light stands for life, purity, holiness, the kingdom of God. Darkness, by contrast, stands for sin, unbelief, death, and the realm of the demonic and satanic. We have been called "out of darkness into his marvellous light," says Peter (I Pet. 2:9). Or, in the words of Paul, "Once you were darkness, but now in the Lord you are light" (Eph. 5:8).

In Judaism Adam, the Torah and important rabbis were described as light-bearers in the world. In Daniel 12:3 we read of people in the resurrection age who "will shine as lights in the brightness of the heavens, and those who lead many to righteousness, as stars." By their godly life, by their witness, by spreading the good news of the gospel, believers illuminate the world in which they live.

In order to fulfil their mission here on earth, the readers are to remain faithful to the word of life. "It is by your holding fast to the word of life," says Paul, that they can be true light-bearers. The verb "to hold fast" can also mean "to hold forth" (*epecho*). Translators are not agreed on which meaning to follow. The Good News Bible, for example, reads, "as you offer them the message of life." In that case,

Paul is stressing the missionary calling of the church, in line with verse 15. But it is quite possible the apostle wants to point out to his readers what they must do in order to shine as stars in a dark sky: "holding fast to the word of life."

The participle "holding fast" suggests this is an ongoing activity. To "hold fast" would mean, among other things, that the readers remain loyal and faithful to the message of the gospel. In fact, if they did not "hold fast" the word of life, they would hardly be in a position to "hold forth" the good news. "Word of life" is just another of the many ways in which the gospel message is designated. It is a message about the new life that can be had in Christ, if one accepts the gospel. It is a message that creates new life when it is embraced by faith and obedience. The gospel is the good news "about this new life" (Acts 5:20), that is, eternal life, the life of the age to come, which those who believe can enjoy as a foretaste in the here and now.

If the Philippians continue to hold fast the word of life and if they continue to shine as stars in this dark world, then Paul is sure his labors will not be in vain. "That I can boast on the day of Christ that I did not run in vain or labor in vain." Paul always viewed his apostolic ministry in the light of the great day at the end of the age when he, together with all the saints, would stand before God. He has already mentioned this day several times (1:6,10; 2:10,11) and will refer to it again in 3:20.

Assuming that the readers will be faithful in their Christian life and calling, Paul will have reason to boast on that last day. Paul can hardly be accused of vanity when he speaks of "boasting," for the word to boast is a religious word meaning to praise, to glory, to exult. "Let the one who boasts, boast in the Lord," he wrote to the Corinthians (I Cor. 1:31), quoting words from Jeremiah.

"The day of Christ" is the day when Paul will have to give account of his stewardship. "The day of Christ" is a combination found only here and in 1:10. Elsewhere it is "the day of Jesus Christ," "the last day," "the great day" or simply "the day." All these expressions have their background in the Old Testament "day of the Lord."

On that great day Paul hopes it will be confirmed "that he did not run in vain or labor in vain." Paul often uses athletic figures of speech, and here we have the word "run," which describes his ministry as a whole. To run not only stresses the effort and strain of Paul's missionary endeavors, but there is also the emphasis of attaining to the goal. To run in vain would be a way of saying that a runner had not reached his or her goal. The servant of the Lord in Isaiah 49:4 complained that he had "labored in vain." Paul does not want to labor in vain. And so a second metaphor is added to that of "run" to describe his missionary efforts.

The word for "labor" *(kopiao)* stresses the exertion, even the weariness, that accompanies missionary work. The noun *kopos* (labor) came to be used regularly for missionary activity in the early centuries of the Christian church. When the last day comes Paul does not want to appear empty-handed before his Lord. He wants to hear the Lord's "well done" at the end of life.

V. THE PERSONAL EXAMPLE (vv. 17,18)

"But even if I am being poured out as a libation over the sacrifice and the offering of your faith, I am glad and rejoice with all of you—and in the same way you also must be glad and rejoice with me." The imagery now changes and Paul looks upon his life and ministry as a sacrifice. The suffering of the apostle for the sake of his converts would certainly touch a tender spot in the hearts of the Philippians. Personal examples of dedication and sacrifice exercise a strong influence over others. Paul not only puts forth strenuous efforts in his ministry, but he is willing even to die for the sake of Christ and the gospel. "Even if I am poured out" points to the possibility of the apostle's death as a martyr. He thinks of his death as a libation or drink-offering which is poured out over or beside the altar. When a burnt offering or cereal offering was presented at the altar of Israel's sanctuary, a drink-offering of wine or olive oil might be poured over or beside it. It completed the offering.

Similarly Paul thinks of his life-blood being poured out, not literally, but in the sense of yielding his life to God as a sacrifice. Like his Lord (2:8) he is willing to be obedient to his calling to the point of death. This sacrifice of his life for the gospel will be like a drink-offering poured out "over the sacrifice and offering" of the faith of the Philippians. He gives his life as an added sacrifice for his readers. The word "sacrifice" (*thusia*) is well known in the LXX. Service (*leitourgia*) is conjoined here with sacrifice. In secular usage *leitourgia* meant any kind of public service. In the LXX it is used for the service of priests and levites in the temple. In the New Testament however, all of God's people are priests, and so the word is used noncultically of service rendered to meet the needs of other people. In 2 Corinthians 9:12 it is used to designate the collection for the poor in Jerusalem. Perhaps it is best if sacrifice and service in our text were viewed as one concept: "sacrificial service."

But what does he mean with the sacrificial service "of your faith?" One might read the expression as indicating the source of their service; their faith provided the impulse for their sacrificial service. If read epexegetically, "the faith" itself is the sacrificial service. In that case, we would have to understand "faith" in a more concrete sense, as the life of faith—their daily life as Christians in a world which often was very hard for believers. Included in this life of faith would be their financial contributions to the work of the kingdom, their intercession for others and their efforts to spread the gospel.

It appears as if Paul thinks the sacrificial service of the Philippians as being the major offering made to God. His own sacrifice, like a drink-offering poured out in addition to the main offering, is of lesser significance. It is added simply to complete their own sacrifice.

Paul is not complaining about his lot, his suffering, his heavy labors, his poverty. Sacrifice for the sake of the kingdom and profound joy are not mutually exclusive. "I am glad and rejoice with all of you—and in the same way you also must be glad and rejoice with me." Not only does he rejoice at the fact that he himself is sacrificing his life for the cause of Christ, but also that the Philippians share with him in both the sacrifice and the joy. Not only does he recognize their joy but he exhorts them to continue to rejoice. Paul at this point piles up words of "joy." Twelve times in this letter Paul uses the verb "rejoice" and six times the word "joy." Could it be that the lack of joy in modern Christianity stems from our unwillingness to sacrifice for the sake of Christ and his kingdom?

Review Questions

1. *Mention some practical ways in which believers can "work out" their salvation.*

2. *Why is obedience so important in the Christian life?*

3. *How can we overcome the temptation to grumble and complain?*

4. *What does it mean in our day to be without reproach in a crooked and perverse society?*

5. *How can we be lights in a dark world?*

6. *What difference would it make in our lives if we learned to live in the light of the coming day of Christ?*

7. *Mention some sacrifices we could make for the sake of the gospel.*

CHAPTER EIGHT

Paul's Immediate Plans (2:19-30)

I hope in the Lord Jesus to send Timothy to you soon, so that I may be cheered by news of you. I have no one like him who will be genuinely concerned for your welfare. All of them are seeking their own interests, not those of Jesus Christ. But Timothy's worth you know, how like a son with a father he has served with me in the work of the gospel. I hope therefore to send him as soon as I see how things go with me; and I trust in the Lord that I will also come soon. Still, I think it necessary to send to you Epaphroditus — my brother and co-worker and fellow soldier, your messenger and minister to my need; for he has been longing for all of you, and has been distressed because you heard that he was ill. He was indeed so ill that he nearly died. But God had mercy on him, and not only on him but on me also, so that I would not have one sorrow after another. I am the more eager to send him, therefore, in order that you may rejoice at seeing him again, and that I may be less anxious. Welcome him then in the Lord with all joy, and honor such people, because he came close to death for the work of Christ, risking his life to make up for those services that you could not give me (Philippians 2:19-30).

This paragraph, wedged between Paul's profound christological confession (2:5-11) and the warnings of chapter 3, has often been treated as if it had little significance for the church. The modern reader might be tempted to ask: what do Paul's travel plans for two of his friends have to do with our life in the world today? However, we would be poorer if we did not have these "travelogues" of Paul found here and there throughout his correspondence with the churches.

Paul is in prison; he does not yet know what the outcome of his trial will be. He would very much like to visit the Philippians, but that is impossible at the moment. And so he sends two of his co-workers, Epaphroditus, who had come from Philippi, and Timothy, his faithful companion, to his friends in Philippi.

As we survey this short travelogue two outstanding examples of Christ's servants take on shape and form. And just as Paul's portrait of Christ (2:5-11) was designed to motivate the Christian reader, these two snapshots of men who stand out in their devotion to Christ, challenge us twentieth-century readers to follow in their steps.

There is nothing quite so inspiring in the Christian life as good models. The British churchman, Dean Inge, once made the comment "It does not seem to me that clever books and brilliant sermons have done so much for me as those chance glimpses into characters far above our own." Paul gives us glimpses of two characters which we must learn to emulate.

It should perhaps also be noted that Paul keeps on making plans even though the possibility of martyrdom stares him in the face. As long as God gives him breath he does what is within his power, to participate in the ongoing work of the kingdom of God. Let us now turn to Paul's plans for his younger co-worker, Timothy.

I. HIS PLANS FOR TIMOTHY (vv. 19-24)

A. The Statement of the Plan (v. 19a)
"I hope in the Lord Jesus to send Timothy to you soon." Paul's future is not certain. But as he awaits his trial he expresses the hope of sending Timothy to Philippi shortly. Usually when Paul uses the

word "hope" it has an eschatological meaning, but in several letters he uses the word in connection with his travel plans (Rom. 15:24; 1 Cor. 16:7; Philemon 22). Hope in our text is a rough equivalent for "wish" or "plan."

That sounds very human and earthly, but we should never think lightly of the human dimensions in our service and life as Christians. However, Paul expresses the desire to have Timothy visit the Philippians "in the Lord Jesus." Paul does not make plans like a worldly person who lives independently of God. His plans are subject to the orderings of divine providence, guidance and even overruling. On an earlier occasion, when he planned to send Timothy from Ephesus to Corinth, Paul added "if the Lord wills" (I Cor. 4:19). He does not use those words here but they are implied in the words "in the Lord Jesus." He lives in fellowship with Jesus Christ and his hopes and plans are subject to his will.

Paul does not yet know when he will send Timothy, for he makes the timing dependent on the outcome of his own trial ("as soon as I see how things go with me," v. 23).

B. The Reason for the Plan (v. 19b)
"So that I may be cheered by news of you." The Philippians no doubt were anxious to hear how Paul was doing. Paul, on the other hand, is concerned about the welfare of his readers and will be greatly encouraged when he hears from them. And so he slips in the words "I also." Timothy's visit then, will have a twofold purpose. The Philippians will be cheered up by news about Paul, and Paul will be uplifted by hearing about them.

The word *eupsucheo* (be glad, have courage, cheer up) is found only here in the New Testament. It has been found on gravestones in ancient Greece where it means something like "be it well with your soul."

This is not the only occasion when Paul sent his faithful coworker to carry out a mission which the apostle himself could not fulfill. These assignments offered little in terms of pleasure or material rewards. There were no jet planes to board or Hiltons to stay at overnight. Some of these missions were downright dangerous. But Timothy was willing to serve at great risk. To be willing to be sent, to take on special assignments in the life of the church, calls for genuine devotion to the cause of Christ.

C. The Elaboration of the Plan (vv. 20-24)

1. Timothy's Concern (vv. 20,21). "I have no one like him who will be genuinely concerned for your welfare. All of them are seeking their own interests, not those of Jesus Christ."

The reason Paul is asking Timothy to go to Philippi is simply because he has no one else available with such a concern for the church as Timothy. "For I have no one equal in soul." There is a wordplay here. Paul has just used the word *eupsucheo* and now says he has no one who is so *isopsuchos* (similar in soul). Again the word is found only here in the New Testament. Timothy is, as it were, Paul's alter ego; he will represent the apostle well. In his concern for the Philippians Timothy is Paul's equal.

Timothy is genuinely concerned about the welfare of the Philippians. Quite literally, he "worries" about the church. The word "worry" (*merimnao*) is used in both a bad and a good sense. In 4:6 Paul exhorts his readers not to worry; but here the word is used in the sense of loving care and concern for the welfare of the readers. And this concern is "genuine" (the word *gnesios* originally meant legitimate, but here it means sincerely, genuinely).

His concern for the Philippians is seen even more clearly when compared with those who "are seeking their own interests, not those of Jesus Christ" (v. 21). When Paul says that others "all" seek their own interests, the "all" must not be taken in the absolute sense. One could read it as hyperbole to enhance the selfless spirit of Timothy. Or it could be a general remark on the selfishness found everywhere in the world. The word "all" obviously does not include those Christians in Rome who are sympathetic to Paul's concern and who would otherwise be willing to go on this mission.

If Luke and Aristarchus, who went to Rome with Paul, had still been with the apostle, he could hardly have used the word "all" in such a comprehensive way. Evidently there was no one immediately available whom Paul could trust with this mission to Philippi.

2. Timothy's Character (v. 22). "But Timothy's worth you know; how like a son with a father he has served with me in the work of the gospel." After contrasting Timothy with others who were self-seeking, Paul gives another reason why he wants to send Timothy: the Philippians know his worth. The word *dokime* means tested and tried and then to be approved. Timothy has a proven character. The apostle is not sending an untried novice. Timothy was with Paul when he founded the Philippian church and they had learned to know him at that time. In contrast to John Mark who cut short his mission with Paul and Barnabas, Timothy had stuck with Paul through thick and thin and the readers must have heard about this faithful servant from time to time.

In I Corinthians 4:17 Paul speaks of Timothy as his beloved and faithful son, very much like he does here: "Like a son with a father he has served with me." The word to serve (*douleuo*) is taken from the realm of slavery. Timothy "slaved" with Paul in the work of the gospel. Paul is careful not to say that Timothy served "him;" rather, he served "with him." There was genuine collegiality between an older Paul and a younger Timothy.

That Paul should call Timothy his "child" should not surprise us, for Paul had led Timothy to the Lord (I Cor. 4:17; 2 Tim. 1:2). Moreover, it was not at all unusual for rabbis to call their students "sons." Paul here uses the language of spiritual parenthood to describe the relationship of Timothy to himself. Jointly they labored in the great cause of furthering the gospel.

3. Paul's Circumstances (vv. 23,24). "I hope therefore to send him as soon as I see how things go with me; and I trust in the Lord that I will also come soon."

The language of verse 23 resembles that of verse 19, except that it is a bit more precise. The promise to send Timothy "soon" is qualified by "as soon as I see how things go with me." Most exegetes understand this explanation to be a reference to Paul's trial. As soon as Paul knows which way the verdict will go, Timothy will be on his way. Why Timothy needed to stay in Rome while Paul awaited the verdict is not known. There may have been pastoral duties that Timothy needed to attend to while Paul was kept in prison.

However, Paul not only hopes to send his faithful emissary, but he himself plans to come as well. He expresses confidence in the Lord that he will be able to come soon. It is another way of saying, "If it's the Lord's will." But before either Timothy or even Paul can go to Philippi, one of their own members, Epaphroditus, will be coming to them any day.

II. HIS PLANS FOR EPAPHRODITUS (vv. 25-30)

A. The Statement of the Plan (v. 25)

"Still, I think it necessary to send to you Epaphroditus—my brother and coworker and fellow-soldier, your messenger and minister to my need." The portraits of two of Paul's fellow-workers, Timothy and Epaphroditus, manifest the apostle's great capacity for friendship. He is not hesitant to heap expressions of admiration and appreciation upon those who devoted their lives to the work of God's kingdom. For us twentieth-century readers Epaphroditus remains an inspiring example of self-sacrificing service.

Epaphroditus is mentioned only in Paul's letter to the Philippians. We know nothing about his background. His family may have been worshippers of the goddess Aphrodite (from whom his name is derived). Epaphras is a shortened form of the name, but the two are not one and the same person (Col. 1:7; 4:12). We know Epaphroditus was a member of the Philippian church and he had brought help to Paul from his home congregation. He is about to return to Philippi and should be thought of as the bearer of Paul's letter to the church at Philippi. Private letters had to be delivered by private messengers since the imperial post carried only official correspondence. If the text is read as if Epaphroditus is already on the way home, then of course he could not have been the bearer of this letter.

Before Paul tells his readers why Epaphroditus had not come back sooner, he outdoes himself in commending this faithful Philippian messenger. He bestows five honorable titles on this servant of God.

1. My Brother. The pronoun "my" should be read with the first three titles, and these three titles all appear under one definite article. "Brother " is Paul's favorite word for "Christian." Believers thought of themselves as belonging to the same family and called each other brother or sister (a practice that gave rise to criticisms by non-church people who accused Christians of illegitimate intimacies) .

2. My Fellow-worker. Whereas "brother" was a word used for believers in general, this cannot be said of the word *sunergos* (fellow-worker). Paul seems to be moving from the general to the more specific. The apostle uses this title about a dozen times in his correspondence to designate those who shared with him the ministry of the gospel.

3. My Fellow-soldier. From the familial and the collegial Paul switches to a military metaphor. Military terms are common for Paul since he thought of his ministry as a battle with evil powers that are bent on destroying God's work. The title "fellow-soldier" is found only here and in Philemon 2. Paul seems to delight in words that are compounded by the preposition *sun* (together). Although the apostle was a pioneer in many respects, he did not think of himself as a lone ranger. He delighted in the fact that he could stand shoulder to shoulder with other soldiers of the cross.

The story is told of Lienhard Bleuler, an Anabaptist farmer, who was asked by the judge to give up his faith. Bleuler responded, "I am God's servant and no longer my own boss and cannot make my own decisions. I have enlisted with Jesus Christ who is my General, and will stay with him even unto death, and whatever he commands I will do obediently." No doubt he had learned to use that kind of language from reading the New Testament.

What conflicts and adversaries Epaphroditus had faced in the spiritual warfare he was engaged in is not known. Persecution and all kinds of trials for the sake of the Christian faith may have been in Paul's mind. Perhaps he had even shared Paul's imprisonment. In any case, he had suffered in his efforts to deliver the gift of the Philippians, and so he can justifiably be called a "fellow-soldier."

4. Your Messenger. Whereas the first three titles speak of Epaphroditus' relationship with Paul, the last two describe his relationship with his own church. The word "messenger" is *apostolos*— a word used in a special sense of the Twelve disciples and of others, like Paul, who were divinely commissioned by the risen Christ. Here, however, it is used in its more general sense of "envoy" ,"representative," "messenger" (for a similar use see 2 Cor. 8:23). Our word "missionary" might be a good current rendering of this meaning of *apostolos*, for a missionary is one who is sent out on a mission as a representative, an envoy of his or her church.

5. Your Minister of My Need. Perhaps this last title should be read together with the previous in the sense of "your messenger sent to minister to my need." The noun *leitourgos* (liturgy) is derived from the word *laos* (people) and *ergon* (work), a person who works for the good of the community, a benefactor. In the LXX the word is used for the service of priests and Levites in the temple. Although there is no priestly class in the New Testament church, it may well be that Paul uses the word to describe the ministry of the gospel as a priestly service to God.

But what does "minister of my need" mean? That would most certainly include bringing the gift of the Philippians to Paul in Rome. But it may be that Epaphroditus was expected by his congregation to minister to Paul in other ways, for Paul seems to apologize for sending him back. It almost appears as if the Philippians had put Epaphroditus at Paul's disposal, but because of his illness and other reasons, Paul is now sending him back. Paul expands on the reasons for the return of Epaphroditus in the next verses.

B. The Reason for the Plan (vv. 26-28)
"For he has been longing for all of you, and has been distressed because you heard that he was ill. He was indeed so ill that he nearly died. But God had mercy on him, and not only on him but on me also, so that I would not have one sorrow after another. I am the more eager to send him, therefore, in order that you may rejoice at seeing him again, and that I may be less anxious."

At least two reasons for the return of Epaphroditus are mentioned explicitly; there may have been others. One was his longing for his friends back home; and the other, his distress over their concerns for him. Whether Epaphroditus had fallen sick on his way to Rome or while in Rome is not clear. Some unknown traveler must have conveyed this sad message to the Philippian believers and they were worried about their messenger. These worries of his friends back home in turn disturbed Epaphroditus so much he was willing to return.

However, there was another reason for his willingness to go home: he was homesick for his friends. And lest anyone in the church should feel left out, Paul stresses that their envoy longed to see "all" of them (some manuscripts in fact add the verb "to see"). The mental distress of Epaphroditus is underscored by the use of a second verb which speaks of great mental anxiety. It is the verb that is used to describe Christ's anguish in Gethsemane (Mk. 14:33). The verb *ademoneo* means basically "not at home" (*unheimlich*, as said in German). If all of this sounds a bit sentimental to us, then we have probably misunderstood what Paul is trying to say. Epaphroditus, like Timothy, was a man who was genuinely concerned about his home church. One can hardly imagine what our churches today would be like if all the members of the congregation had such sincere love and concern for each other.

Paul now confirms what the Philippians had heard. Epaphroditus had been sick; in fact, he had been deathly ill. To put it literally, "he was the next door neighbor to death." If there should be a question in the minds of some Philippians about the early return of their representative, this information should put such suspicions to rest. And his restoration to health was nothing short of an act of mercy on God's part. Paul gives no information on how Epaphroditus was restored. Was it an answer to prayer, the laying on of hands for healing, the result of some medicine? We do not know; the emphasis lies on God's mercy. In Paul's other writings, God's mercy is mentioned more often in connection with God's activity in bringing about the salvation of humanity. But in the Gospels, and also in this particular text, it is related to physical need. God had intervened on behalf of Epaphroditus and saved him from death.

The restoration of Epaphroditus was for Paul not only an act of sovereign mercy in the life of his faithful coworker, but it was also an expression of mercy manifested towards Paul himself. Had Epaphroditus died, one sorrow would have piled upon another in Paul's heart. But God lavished his mercy on the apostle so he might be spared one grief after another. Paul had enough grief to contend with as it was—his adversaries and his imprisonment. God spared him a second wave of sorrow by restoring Epaphroditus. Had this servant of God passed away Paul no doubt would have humbly bowed to the sovereign will of God, but that did not mean Paul was a Stoic without feelings. It is not fair to expect believers to live constantly on cloud nine; they weep and mourn too.

Now that Epaphroditus is feeling better again, Paul is all the more eager to send him back to Philippi (v. 28). The past tense of "send" (*aorist*) is epistolary, meaning from the standpoint of the readers it is past but from the standpoint of the writer it is present. Paul is now sending him back as quickly as possible. Epaphroditus will then answer all their questions and also convey Paul's thanks for their gift. And when they see Epaphroditus the Philippians will rejoice and he will be less sorrowful. Their joy had turned to sadness when they heard their envoy had fallen ill; it would now be restored. Also, Paul himself will be less anxious once Epaphroditus is back home. Not that his circumstances will improve, for surely he will miss Epaphroditus, but he will not have to worry about the Philippians any longer. The sorrow caused by his incarceration will of course remain, as will the attacks by his adversaries.

C. The Response to the Plan (vv. 29,30)
"Welcome him then in the Lord with all joy, and honor such people, because he came close to death for the work of Christ, risking his life to make up for those services that you could not give me."
1. The Manner (v. 29a). Paul exhorts his readers to welcome Epaphroditus wholeheartedly when he arrives. They are to welcome him "in the Lord." Precisely what that means is not clear. If we connect this phrase with the verb "welcome," Paul may be saying they should receive Epaphroditus as the Lord would welcome him. If "in the Lord" is connected with "with all joy" it could be understood as meaning they should receive him in the characteristic Christian way. "In the Lord" could also refer to the fellowship which both the Philippians and Epaphroditus have in Christ, i.e., as a brother in the Lord (as in the GNB).
The expression "with all joy" suggests the church should receive their envoy back without any reserve, wholeheartedly, gladly. Behind this exhortation one senses a concern of Paul that some Philippians may have been somewhat resentful that Epaphroditus had not stayed on to minister to Paul's needs.
2. The Admonition (v. 29b). "Hold such people in honor." People like Epaphroditus are worthy of respect and esteem in the church. Paul says something very similar about the house of Stephanas in his

letter to the Corinthians (I Cor. 16:15). Jesus had taught that those who serve are the greatest in the kingdom of God (Mk. 10:42-45) and Epaphroditus had done this.

The adjective *entimos* can mean precious, prized, honored, valuable. Here the apostle admonishes his readers to value people like Epaphroditus and honor them. In I Thessalonians 5:12 Paul exhorts the Thessalonians to esteem their leaders highly "because of their work." In the case of Epaphroditus, he was worthy of honor not only because of the work he had done but also because of the sacrifice he had brought.

3. The Incentive (v. 30). "Because he came close to death for the work of Christ, risking his life to make up for those services that you could not give me." In his attempt to fulfill his mission Epaphroditus nearly lost his life. In the early church those who had suffered for the cause of Christ were always held in high regard; sometimes, in fact, their authority was greater than that of other church leaders.

Paul uses colorful language to characterize the efforts of Epaphroditus. He "gambled" with his life. The verb *paraboleuomai* means to gamble, to hazard, to expose oneself to danger. The word *psuche* (soul) here means "life." We do not know exactly which risks he took when he went on his journey to Rome to serve Paul. Travel as such was often quite hazardous in those days. For example, Paul mentions the danger of bandits (2 Cor. 11:26).

There were people in the early church who were called *parabolanoi*. These were Christians who risked their lives to nurse those sick from plagues. In the Decian persecution (A.D. 252) a plague broke out in Carthage and the pagans threw out the bodies of the dead and fled in terror. Cyprian the bishop gathered his congregation and they set about to bury the dead and nurse the dying at the risk of catching the disease.

There were services the Philippians would have been glad to perform for Paul, but their distance from Rome made this impossible. By sending Epaphroditus to Rome they made up for what they could not give in the person of their representative. Paul tactfully acknowledges that he had needs and he is careful not to criticize the readers for any neglect on their part. Epaphroditus brought their gift to Rome and did what he could for Paul while in that city. Earlier (v. 25) Paul had called Epaphroditus a *leitourgos* (servant, minister); now he calls his service a *leitourgia*.

Two snapshots of servants of Christ who inspire us even today to self-sacrifice and humble service in the kingdom of God! I am reminded of a news reporter who used to cover the preaching services of the great homiletition, John Broadus, of Southern Baptist Seminary in Louisville. After hearing Broadus preach again and again, he confessed that he always went away wanting to be a better person. That is how one feels after looking at these two ministers of the first-century church.

Review Questions

1. *How did Paul, Timothy and Epaphroditus show their love for the church? What can we learn from them in this regard?*

2. *Is there a place for friendship in the church in view of the fact that we are all members of the same family?*

3. *What can we learn from this passage about relationships between senior and junior members of the church?*

4. *Why does Paul use military metaphors (see v. 25) to describe the work of God's servants?*

5. *What should be the attitude of a congregation to its envoys who serve on their behalf, often in distant lands?*

6. *Can you think of representatives of the church who are risking their lives today in order to carryout the church's mandate?*

CHAPTER NINE

Pastoral Concerns (3:1-7)

Finally, my brothers and sister, rejoice in the Lord. To write the same things to you is not troublesome to me, and for you it is a safeguard. Beware of the dogs, beware of the evil workers, beware of those who mutilate the flesh! For it is we who are the circumcision, who worship in the Spirit of God and boast in Christ Jesus and have no confidence in the flesh — even though I, too, have reason for confidence in the flesh. If anyone else has reason to be confident in the flesh, I have more: circumcised on the eighth day, a member of the people of Israel, of the tribe of Benjamin, a Hebrew born of Hebrews; as to the law, a Pharisee; as to zeal, a persecutor of the church; as to righteousness under the law, blameless. Yet whatever gains I had, these I have come to regard as loss because of Christ (Philippians 3:1-7).

The word "finally" with which this chapter begins could be understood as indicating the letter was coming to a close. However, Paul is about to make a great digression in which he will treat the special dangers facing the church at Philippi and to teach his readers how to face these threats to their faith.

Some scholars take chapter 3 to be an interpolation. In fact, it has been suggested this chapter has been inserted by someone other than Paul. Granted, there is a marked change of tone in this chapter, but it is not all that unusual for Paul to make abrupt turns in his train of thought. Some English Bibles take 3:1 to be the last verse of chapter 2, because it does not seem to fit the tone of what immediately follows (e.g., NRSV). There were, of course, no chapter divisions in Paul's letters.

"Finally," however, does not necessarily indicate that Paul is about to conclude his letter. *To loipon* (finally) literally means "as for the rest" and can be read as a transitional statement, introducing a new section. Perhaps if we render it as "and now" or "well then" we would not be wide of the mark.

In the paragraph we are about to study Paul expresses some pastoral concerns. Specifically he warns the congregation against legalism and, to strengthen his case, he becomes autobiographical, recounting his own past life in Judaism and confessing that all his past efforts to make himself acceptable to God had led him to spiritual bankruptcy. We want to divide the text into two parts: Paul's pastoral instructions (vv. 1-3), and his pastoral confessions (vv. 4-7).

I. PASTORAL INSTRUCTIONS (vv. 1-3)

A. On the Mood of the Christian Life (v. 1a)

"Finally, my brothers, rejoice in the Lord." Although the verb "rejoice" (*chairete*) can also mean "farewell" (as in 2 Cor. 13:11; see NRSV), that does not seem to be the meaning here. The call to rejoice is repeated in 4:4 and the translation "good-bye" would certainly not fit that context either. The note of joy has been struck repeatedly in the letter so far, and since joy is characteristic of the Christian life we are not surprised to find it in the context of our text. In fact, joy may be seen as the best antidote against legalism, which does not make for a joyful Christian life.

The call to rejoice is not an exhortation to put plastic smiles on our faces, for Christian joy can be experienced in the midst of pain and suffering. Paul could rejoice (1:18) even when his enemies were rubbing salt into his wounds. He rejoices even as he faces martyrdom (2:17).

In our text Paul calls upon his readers ("brothers" is used here in the ecclesiastical sense of church members) to rejoice "in the Lord." Even though this phrase is not always attached to the word "rejoice," it is implied, for the joy that Paul has in mind throughout this letter is joy in the Lord, i.e., Christian joy. Although the Lord could be seen as the object of the believer's joy, more likely the meaning is that the Christian's joy rises out of fellowship with Christ, the Lord.

B. On the Value of Apostolic Traditions (v. 1b)

"To write the same things to you is not troublesome to me, and for you it is a safeguard." Precisely what Paul had in mind when he wrote "the same things" is not altogether clear. Some take the phrase to refer to other letters which Paul may have written to the Philippians. We do not have such letters, but in Polycarp's letter to the Philippians (Ad Phil. 3:2), the bishop of Smyrna mentions that Paul used to write letters to them.

Others take "the same things" to refer to the repeated exhortation to rejoice (1:25; 2:18,28,29). But if that were the meaning, why would Paul apologize for repeating himself? However, he does add that repeated exhortations make the Philippians safe.

Perhaps it is best to understand "the same things" to be a reference to earlier exhortations regarding the Christian life which are sprinkled throughout the previous chapters. Paul knows the believers need to be exhorted again and again to live the Christian way in this world, and so it does not trouble him when he repeats himself, for he knows it makes his readers more firm in the faith.

These exhortations are called apostolic "traditions." We usually use the word "tradition" in a pejorative sense, but it also has a positive meaning. Paul praises the Corinthians for maintaining "the traditions just as I handed them on to you " (I Cor. 11:2). Apostolic teachings, both doctrinal and ethical, are called traditions. The apostles thought of themselves as God's servants who passed on to the next generation the teachings which ultimately have their roots in Jesus. In our day, in which there is little appreciation for the past, it is important for Christians to remember that if we neglect the apostolic traditions, we lose our way.

94 A Testament Of Joy

C. On the Dangers of Legalism (v. 2)

"Beware of the dogs, beware of the evil workers, beware of those who mutilate the flesh." Somewhat abruptly Paul uses the imperative "beware" three times in close succession to warn his readers against "dogs" (*kunas*), "evil workers" (*kakous ergatas*) and "the mutilation" (*katatome*)—three words beginning with the letter "k."

Dogs were regarded as unclean animals in those days because of what they ate. Paul does not have domesticated pups in mind but scavengers that used to prowl through the streets of the cities of the ancient world. It was a contemptuous word used by Jews to speak of Gentiles, for the latter did not submit to Jewish dietary laws. With irony Paul turns the spear around and uses the epithet "dogs" for the Judaizers. Paul had a deep love for his people, the Jews (see Rom. 9:3), but when false teachers tried to lead Christians to a legalistic way of life, he thought they deserved to be called what Jews regularly called Gentiles, namely "dogs."

The epithet "evil workers" can be found in the Psalter (5:5; 6:8; etc.) where it describes the enemies of the Psalmist. In our text "workers" may be a reference to the missionary activity on the part of the Judaizers (i.e., Judaizing Christians or members of the Jewish synagogue). Paul describes their work as evil because they are seeking to win over the Philippians to a way of life that was contrary to the gospel message Paul had preached.

Others take "evil workers" to be a reference to people who are seeking to be justified by "the works of the law." Paul calls them evil, not because they live immorally or have deceitful designs, but because they trust in the works of the law for salvation. However, it is more likely Paul has the Judaizers in mind.

Paul gives these people the derogatory epithet of "mutilation." The word *katatome* is a play on the word *peritome* (circumcision). The term is not found anywhere else in the Bible, but evidently Paul did not want to call them "the circumcision"—the sacred seal of God's covenant with Israel. It is probably best to read this as a pun, in which Paul mockingly calls circumcision a mutilation, a cutting on the body.

Already in the Old Testament the prophets had pointed out that circumcision as such was insufficient to make one a member of the true people of God; one also needed to be circumcised in the heart, ears and mouth (Dt. 10:16; Jer. 4:4; Ez. 44:7). This spiritual kind of circumcision, of course, was not to take the place of the circumcision of the flesh. In the New Testament church, however, circumcision is no longer of any significance. "For neither circumcision nor uncircumcision is anything; but a new creation is everything" (Gal. 6:15).

Paul is not denouncing the practice of circumcision in general. Jewish Christians continued to circumcise their sons even after they became members of the Christian church. However, as we can see from the decision made at the Jerusalem Council (Acts 15), circumcision, which was the source of pride in Jewish history, played no part in the gospel of salvation by grace and was not a requirement for membership in the new people of God, the church. Paul's denunciations are aimed at those who came into Christian churches, such as Philippi, and insisted that circumcision was necessary for salvation. Such people have been given the opprobrious name of "Judaizers."

D. On the Marks of True Believers (v. 3)

"For it is we who are the circumcision, who worship in the Spirit of God and boast in Christ Jesus and have no confidence in the flesh." In contrast to the three opprobrious epithets for those who represent a distortion of the Christian faith, Paul gives three marks of the true people of God, the church. He latches onto the last of the three epithets, the mutilation, and claims that Christians are the true circumcision, the covenant people. The church has entered into Israel's heritage. Paul thinks of Christian believers as "true Jews," not Jews after the flesh but after the Spirit (Rom. 2:25-29); indeed, they are the "Israel of God" (Gal. 6:16). Because this is so, Peter can call Christians "a chosen race, a royal priesthood, a holy nation, God's own people" (I Pet. 2:9)—titles used to designate Old Testament Israel, but now carried over to the church. And what are the marks of those who have been circumcised with the "circumcision of Christ?"

1. They Worship in the Spirit of God (v. 3a). There are some manuscripts and ancient versions that make God the object of the worship: "We worship God in the Spirit." But the word "worship" (*latreuo*) does not need an object, for it means to worship God in any case. In the LXX this verb describes the service rendered to God by his people Israel. Now Paul claims it is the church that worships God. And it does so with the help of the Spirit of God.

We should not limit the verb "worship" to the formal aspects of worship such as prayer, teaching, the breaking of bread and so forth, for *latreuo* is a broad enough word to include other services that believers render to God in everyday life. The prophets repeatedly criticize Israel for going through the motions of divine worship when their hearts were far away from God. We too can fall into that trap, and so we need help. God's Spirit is there to help us in our worship/ service. Jesus told the Samaritan woman that because God is Spirit, those who worship him must do so in Spirit and in truth (Jn. 4:24). Whether it is prayer, song, confession or loving service of the needy, we need the help of the Spirit at all times.

2. They Glory in Christ Jesus (v. 3b). True believers boast in Christ Jesus. The verb *kauchaomai* (used thirty-five times by Paul out of thirty-seven occurrences in the New Testament), is common in the Old Testament LXX version. It can be used of proud self-confidence (Gal. 6:13) and characterizes the ungodly (Ps. 42:1; 94:4). But it is also used in the sense of praise. In I Corinthians 1:31, Paul, quoting Jeremiah 9:23,24, writes, "Let the one who boasts, boast in the Lord."

In contrast to the Jew who feels self-confident before God because he keeps his law, the true believer looks away from himself and thanks God for his grace and rejoices that divine mercy has embraced him in spite of his sin and made him or her a child of God. Christ Jesus is the object of the believer's praise and thanks. That is not different from boasting in the cross of Christ (Gal. 6:14), for to boast in Christ Jesus implies that the believer rejoices in the saving work of Christ and thanks him for it.

3. They Have No Confidence in the Flesh (v. 3c). The true believer has good reason to boast in the Lord but not in the flesh. Flesh (*sarx*) is a word found some ninety times in Paul and does not always have the same meaning. Sometimes it means "body" (Gal. 2:20); flesh and blood describe people in contrast to God (I Cor. 15:50) simply as human beings. It has an ethnic meaning when, for example, Paul speaks of Israel "after the flesh" (I Cor. 10:18). Sometimes "flesh" refers to human standards (2 Cor. 5:16), and then it is also used to describe that evil power in our lives that fights against the

Spirit of God (Gal. 5:17).

On the one hand, the believer still lives in the flesh (2 Cor. 10:3) in the sense that he or she lives in a body; on the other hand, we are not in the flesh but in the Spirit (Rom. 8:8,9). In our text "flesh" may be a comprehensive term for all those things people put their trust in. However, there seems to be an allusion also to circumcision, in which the Judaizers put so much stock. In the next several verses Paul will list a number of things in which he as a Jew used to put his confidence; among those assets he mentions the fact that he was circumcised on the eighth day. As a true believer now, Paul trusts neither in inherited privilege nor in personal attainments for his salvation.

From these pastoral instructions Paul goes on to make some pastoral confessions. He was a man who had very much trusted in the flesh when he was still an unbeliever, and the following autobiographical reflections are to encourage the readers to stand firm in the faith and not to be tempted by the Judaizers to place their confidence anywhere else except in Christ and his saving work.

II. PASTORAL CONFESSION (vv. 4-7)

A. Paul's Natural Endowments (vv. 4,5)

"Even though I, too, have reason for confidence in the flesh. If anyone else has reason to be confident in the flesh, I have more: circumcised on the eighth day, a member of the people of Israel, of the tribe of Benjamin, a Hebrew born of Hebrews."

1. Circumcised on the Eighth Day. In this brief biographical sketch Paul explains for his readers what it means to have confidence in the flesh. He begins with natural endowments, values that were bestowed upon him by virtue of the fact that he was born into an Orthodox Jewish home. In light of Paul's background, the Judaizers would not be able to hold a candle up to Paul. If anyone ever had reason to put confidence in the flesh it was Paul, and so his criticism of the Judaizers is not simply sour grapes. Paul could outstrip any Judaizer; he had an authentic Jewish background.

Quite literally the Greek text reads, "with respect to circumcision I am an eight day-er." Circumcision was the sign that Paul belonged to the covenant people of God. His parents had strictly adhered to the law and had their son circumcised on the eighth day. Paul was not an Ishmaelite, circumcised in his thirteenth year (Gen. 17:25). Nor was he a proselyte from the Gentiles who took on circumcision when he became a member of the Jewish synagogue. Seven days after his birth Paul's parents had Paul circumcised. He was a true son of Israel.

2. An Israelite by Birth. Paul was not the child of a proselyte; his parents had not been grafted into the covenant people. He was from the original stock. He was of the *genos* (race, stock) of Israel. Whereas the word "Jew" was often used in a derogatory way by Gentiles, the word "Israelite" drew attention to the privileges of belonging to the covenant people. Paul lists some of these privileges in Romans 9:4,5: "They are Israelites, and to them belong the adoption, the glory, the covenants, the giving of the law, the worship, and the promises; to them belong the patriarchs, and from them, according to the flesh, comes the Messiah, who is over all, God blessed forever. Amen."

3. Of the Tribe of Benjamin. Benjamin was the beloved son of Jacob's favorite wife, Rachel. He alone of the twelve patriarchs was born in the promised land. The first king of Israel, Saul, came from the tribe of Benjamin, and Paul had his name. The tribe of Benjamin with Judah formed the core of the community after the return from exile. In Old Testament times Benjamin had a place of honor in battle ("After you, Benjamin," Judges 5:14). Paul could trace his descent from Benjamin and that in itself was considered a high honor. Priests, for example, had to be able to prove their lineage. Paul was not a priest but could trace his lineage.

4. A Hebrew of the Hebrews. This not only means that Paul was of Jewish birth, but that he came from an Orthodox Jewish home in which Aramaic was spoken (although Greek was also known). In other words, they were not "Hellenists" who no longer used the Aramaic language at home and who attended synagogues where Greek was spoken. When Christ revealed himself to Paul on the Damascus Road, he spoke to him in Hebrew (Acts 26:14), which probably means, in its wider sense, Aramaic.

To be a Hebrew of the Hebrews is probably another way of saying that Paul's family tried as much as possible to avoid assimilation into the customs and culture of Tarsus. People may have suspected that Paul, coming from the Diaspora (outside of Palestine) was obviously a Hellenist. Here he explains this was not so. Even though he grew up in a Hellenistic environment, he and his family strictly observed the Jewish way of life . Moreover, his parents had sent him to Jerusalem as a youth to study under Gamaliel to learn the traditions of Orthodox Jewry.

After listing four advantages that Paul had by virtue of his birth and upbringing, he goes on to list three items which could be called personal achievements.

B. Paul's Spiritual Attainments (vv. 5b,6)

1. According to the Law a Pharisee. In the matter of interpreting the Old Testament and observing the law he was a Pharisee. Before the Sanhedrin Paul claimed, "I am a Pharisee, the son of a Pharisee" (Acts 23:6), implying that his father was a Pharisee as well. Moreover, he had studied at the feet of a famous Pharisee, Gamaliel (Acts 5:34). To be a Pharisee meant that Paul had attained to the highest degree of faithfulness in the Jewish faith.

The Pharisees emerged about the second century B.C. as the spiritual heirs of those who had fought to preserve the Jewish traditions when Syrian rulers, such as Antiochus Epiphanes, tried to stamp out the Jewish religion. The word "Pharisee" means "the separated one," and stands for those in Israel whose primary goal was to represent a pure Jewish community. They observed not only the written law as they understood it, but the hundreds of regulations contained in the oral traditions. As a Pharisee Paul had determined that he would walk in the way of holiness.

2. According to Zeal a Persecutor of the Church. Whereas this became a source of great grief to Paul when he became a Christian, it is listed here on the credit side of Paul's achievements. To be zealous for the traditions of the fathers was a sign that Paul was truly devout. Not even his teacher Gamaliel was in favor of persecuting Christians; but Paul went beyond his teacher in this respect.

To be zealous does not mean that Paul had been a member of the Zealot party —political revolutionaries who spearheaded movements to cast off the Roman yoke. Rather, it was the mark of genuine religious devotion. The prototype in this regard was Phinehas (Num. 25:11-13), who in his zeal had stabbed an Israelite engaged in sexual immorality and idolatry.

In Galatians 1:14 Paul calls himself a zealot for the ancestral traditions. In his defence, when he was captured in Jerusalem, he told his Jewish audience he was a zealot for God "as are all of you who are here today" (Acts 22:3). As a Christian Paul saw what a terrible mistake he had made by persecuting the church, and he repented deeply of this sin (1 Tim. 1:13,14). And God forgave him and called him to be his servant. But when he was still devoted to his Jewish faith, he thought he pleased God by persecuting the church.

3. According to Righteousness in the Law, Blameless. This looks like the culmination of all of Paul's spiritual and moral achievements. As far as legal rectitude was concerned Paul had conformed to all the requirements of the law, both written and oral. He could say with the rich young ruler, "All these things have I kept from my youth" (Luke. 18:21). This runs counter to the suggestion that Paul was a tormented man who had serious doubts about his religious faith and who finally broke down on the Damascus Road. From our text we get the impression that Paul was a person quite satisfied with his religious achievements.

In the light of Romans 7 some Bible readers have understood Paul's claim to a blameless life as an ironical statement, but that is not the way to read our text. And it does not mean either that Paul simply "thought" he was blameless, but really was not. "Blameless" means he lived an exemplary life as this was understood in the community in which Paul lived. "Blameless" does not mean sinless but it speaks of scrupulous observance of the law. In other words, Paul was a model Jew.

C. Spiritual Bankruptcy (v. 7)

"Yet whatever gains I had, these I have come to regard as loss because of Christ." Now suddenly all the items listed on the credit side are transferred to the debit side. The heights which Paul had attained to now look abysmal; the pluses have all turned into minuses. The very things which he had counted as gains (he uses accounting terminology) are now seen as losses. Not that the privileges and moral achievements were in themselves evil, but Paul had put his confidence in them; he boasted in them; he depended on them for his acceptance by God.

Because of his conversion to Christ, he now considers (the verb is in the perfect tense, implying a permanent attitude) all his advantages as disadvantages. Having come to know Christ, Paul now sees to his own chagrin that what he at one time considered assets were actually dangers, "fleshly" values in which he had put his confidence. Christ is now worth more to him than anything else in this world.

One might compare Paul to a ship loaded with valuable cargo which the crew throws overboard in stormy weather in order to save the ship and the lives of its crew. Like the man in the Parable of the Pearl (Mt. 13) who discovers a very precious pearl and then sells everything he has to purchase this pearl, so Paul had transferred all his spiritual and moral gains to the debit side of the ledger in order to know Christ. This theme will be expanded on even more in the next paragraph.

Review Questions

1. *What danger threatened the Philippian believers? What are some dangers that threaten the life of the church today?*

2. *Why do we need the help of the Holy Spirit in both our worship of God and in our service during the week?*

3. *What does it mean to "boast" in Christ?*

4. *How can we avoid having "confidence in the flesh?"*

5. *What should our attitude be toward our birth and upbringing?*

6. *How does a person's discovery of Christ "transvaluate all his or her values?"*

CHAPTER TEN

The Transvaluation of All Values (3:8-11)

More than that, I regard everything as loss because of the surpassing value of knowing Christ Jesus my Lord. For his sake I have suffered the loss of all things, and I regard them as rubbish, in order that I may gain Christ and be found in him, not having a righteousness of my own that comes from the law, but one that comes through faith in Christ, the righteousness from God based on faith. I want to know Christ and the power of his resurrection and the sharing of his sufferings by becoming like him in his death, if somehow I may attain the resurrection from the dead (Philippians 3:8-11).

Paul, the Jew from Tarsus, the Pharisee, a Hebrew of the Hebrews, was on his way to Damascus to persecute Christians in that city. On his way there he was suddenly stopped in his path of destruction; the risen Christ appeared to him and called him to be his servant, the bearer of the good news of the gospel. Luke records the story of Paul's conversion three times in the book of Acts. All the values which Paul had held so dearly suddenly lost their attraction; his whole life was turned around; everything was transvalued.

Biblical scholars have often asked what it was that led to such a turnaround in Paul's life. Some critics have suggested psychological explanations. They say Paul, a man with a sensitive conscience, was so tormented by the dastardly things he was doing to Christians, that he had a mental breakdown. But it is hard to believe that a pathological experience should lead to such a fruitful and meaningful life.

Others have tried to explain his conversion on physiological grounds. Paul was a sick man, they say. The thorn in his flesh (2 Cor. 12:7) is taken to be a reference to epileptic fits or something of that nature. But one wonders how a man with such a frail bark and with such a debilitating disease could launch out on such extensive travels by land and sea; how he could endure all the disasters that came his way; how he could work day and night for many years. The picture we get of Paul from the writings of the New Testament is that of a man with considerable stamina.

Still others have given moralistic explanations of Paul's conversion. They describe his turnaround as the climax of a long and profound moral conflict in his soul. Paul loved God's law, it is said, but found out he could not keep it perfectly, no matter how hard he tried. He then externalized this conflict by identifying that which one detests in oneself with another group of people—the Christians—and he found relief in persecuting them. However, from Philippians 3 one does not get the impression that Paul was unhappy with his spiritual and moral attainments. He was not a conscience-smitten man who finally, out of frustration, turned to the Christian faith.

The New Testament documents find the key to the transvaluation of all values in the life of Paul in the divine intervention which he experienced on the road to Damascus. After giving us a long list of his natural endowments and of his spiritual attainments as a devout Orthodox Jew, Paul now explains what it is that has turned everything on its head in his life. He sees his past in a new light; he has different aspirations in the present; and his hope of the future has also changed. We begin with his evaluation of his past in the light of his Christian experience.

I. HIS EVALUATION OF THE PAST (vv. 8,9)

A. The Confession (v. 8a)
"More than that, I regard everything as loss." Paul uses five particles in Greek to introduce this clause: yes, indeed, therefore, at least, even. The translators handle these in different ways: "I would say more" (NEB); "not only that" (JB); "not only those things" (GNB); "yes and more than that" (Bruce). Having introduced the language of gains and losses in verse 7, Paul expands that theme. His earlier decision, mentioned in verse 7, was not a momentary impulsive act which he now regrets. Rather, his deep conviction that his past seems so worthless in the light of his Christian experience has become even more firm.

The word "regard," "consider" (*hegeomai*) is in the perfect tense in verse 7, suggesting a settled conviction. In verse 8, however, he changes over to the present tense to indicate this is a conviction he continues to have. Right up to the present moment he considers all things as loss. "Whatever gains I had" (v. 7) refers to his Jewish advantages. But with the words "all things" (v. 8) he goes beyond his personal achievements and his Jewish heritage. Just what all is included in the "all things" is not spelled out; one might think of his Roman citizenship, material possessions or an assured position in the world (so Peter O'Brian in NIGTC). To put it differently, everything that might stand in the way of his knowledge of Christ is rubbish for Paul.

Throughout the ages there have been those who had similar experiences to that of Paul. Shortly after his conversion Hudson Taylor, the founder of the China Inland Mission, was so overwhelmed by the love of God that he surrendered his life to Christ. This is how he describes the experience: "Well do I remember, as in unreserved consecration I put myself, my life, my friends, my all upon the altar, the deep solemnity that came over my soul with the assurance that my offering was accepted. The presence of God became so unutterably real and blessed; and though under eighteen, I remember stretching myself on the ground, and lying there silent before Him with unspeakable awe and joy. For what service I was accepted I knew not, but a deep consciousness that I was no longer my own took possession of me, which has never since been effaced. It has been a very practical consciousness."

B. The Explanation (v. 8b)

"Because of the surpassing value of knowing Christ Jesus my Lord. For his sake I have suffered the loss of all things, and I regard them as rubbish, in order that I may gain Christ." Paul gave up everything because the knowledge of Christ was so overwhelming. "Christ Jesus" is seen here as the object of knowledge. The knowledge of God is not uncommon in the New Testament, but only here do we have the expression "knowledge of Christ." The word "knowledge" (*gnosis*) must be understood in the Old Testament sense of an intimate and close relationship. "Adam knew his wife" (Gen. 4:1) means he had conjugal relations with her. "To know" sometimes comes close to the meaning of "experience." To know Christ does not mean simply to have information about his life, death, exaltation and so forth; it means, rather to have come to a personal relationship with him. The intimacy of this relationship is underscored by calling him "my Lord."

Paul is not suggesting he has a knowledge of Christ that others do not have but, as Beare puts it, "It would be a dull reader indeed who did not mark the warm and deep devotion which breathes through every phrase." This relationship with Christ is of such surpassing value to Paul that he gladly gave up everything he formerly put his trust and confidence in.

Twice Paul has used the noun "loss" (vv. 7,8); now he adds the verb "to lose," "to forfeit," "to suffer loss" (*zemioo*). He has sustained the loss of everything for the sake of knowing Christ. One can only imagine what it must have cost Paul in terms of his relations with his family, his inheritance, his social standing in Judaism, to throw his lot in with the very people he had persecuted.

The momentous decision he had made when he met Christ on the road to Damascus was confirmed by Paul again and again: "And I regard them as rubbish, in order that I may gain Christ." He has no regrets about the decision he made when he turned to Christ. In fact, the more he thinks of his past the more abhorrent it becomes. The values which he gave up at his conversion were not only "losses," but "rubbish," "dung." This is the only place in the New Testament where this noun occurs (*skubala*). Paul's use of this vulgar term is designed to underscore the force of his total renunciation of all those advantages in which he had formerly put his trust. So strongly does the apostle feel about his past that he abandons the niceties of language. At the risk of embarrassing the reader he speaks of his past values as dung, filth, refuse. Did Paul have Jesus' words in mind when he wrote this line: "What shall it profit a man if he gains the whole world and forfeits his own soul" (Mt. 16:6; Mk. 8:36)?

After his confession (v. 8a) and his explanation (v. 8b), we have a purpose clause which spells out the apostle's anticipation (vv. 8c,9).

C. The Anticipation (vv. 8c,9)

"That I may gain Christ and be found in him, not having a right-eousness of my own that comes from the law, but one that comes through faith in Christ, the righteousness from God based on faith." Again Paul picks up accounting terminology. He has a new purpose in life. He wants to "gain Christ." To gain Christ is not different from knowing Christ. They are simply two different ways of expressing the same purpose and desire. The apostle came to know Christ on his way to Damascus. However, he wants this relationship to deepen; he wants to "gain" Christ. This desire will be fulfilled ultimately in the age to come, but Paul wants to grow in his knowledge of his Lord even in this earthly life.

When the last day comes he wants "to be found in him, not having his own righteousness that comes from the law, but one that comes through faith in Christ, the righteousness from God based on faith." Again Paul is looking forward to the day of Christ when he hopes "to be found in him." Others think the apostle has the day of his death in mind. "To be found in him" is probably a Semitic way of saying "to be in point of fact in Christ."

Paul has no doubt he will be found to be in Christ when this life comes to an end or when Christ returns in glory. He will stand before his Lord not in his own righteousness. In the past Paul had sought to establish his own righteousness that "comes from the law." And he could claim that with respect to the law he had lived a blameless life (v. 6). Writing now as a Christian he sees that in the past he had tried to establish his own righteousness which has no value in the sight of God, and he has thrown this overboard.

In vivid contrast to all self-righteousness stands the righteousness that comes from God, a righteousness which one can obtain only by faith. It has its origin in God; it is offered to us in Christ and it is experienced by faith. God's righteousness is qualitatively different from the righteousness Paul had tried to achieve by being a devout Jew observing the Jewish traditions. The word "righteousness" is not easily understood and I would suggest that when Paul speaks of God's righteousness, which comes to us as a gift of grace, he is thinking of that divine act by which he sets us in the right with God. Perhaps an even simpler way of putting it would be to say that God pardons us. Although we are sinners we can now stand before God as people whose offences have been forgiven.

This new relationship with God is based entirely on his grace; it is not a standing we can earn by doing right. The righteousness we receive from God is a free gift. This gift must, however, be appropriated, and that happens when people put their faith in Christ. "Faith" is not simply a mental assent but involves a personal surrender to Christ. Some scholars take the expression "through faith in Christ" to mean it was through Christ's "faithfulness," through his obedience to the Father in carrying out his plan of salvation, that we have been set right with God. That may be so but verse 9 ends with the phrase "on the basis of faith," and that does appear to speak plainly of the believing, trusting response of those who hear the call of the gospel and commit their lives to Christ.

Having evaluated his past in light of his discovery of Christ, Paul now proceeds to spell out his aspirations in the present (v. 10). To sum up verses 8 and 9, one might say (a) all human beings are alienated from God and need to be put right with him; (b) no one can establish this right relationship by his or her own efforts; (c) God has taken the initiative in restoring our relationship with him; (d) this was an act of grace carried out through Jesus Christ; (e) God's offer of righteousness is found in the gospel; (f) the response to his free gift offered in the gospel is faith. The initial experience of God's grace, when we put our trust in Christ, creates in the believer a desire to know Christ better.

II. HIS ASPIRATIONS IN THE PRESENT (v. 10)

The purpose clauses begun in verses 8 and 9 are continued in verse 10. Paul has the desire to know Christ (the person), the power of his resurrection (the power) and the fellowship of his suffering (the passion). We want to examine verse 10 in this threefold way.

A. The Person

"That I might know him" The verb "to know" is again to be understood in its Hebraic sense of intimate, personal knowledge. Paul has already stated that for the privilege of knowing Christ he had given up everything he had formerly considered as valuable (vv. 6,7). But he is not satisfied with that initial experience; he wants to know Christ better. To know Christ, as has been pointed out, is not different in meaning from "gaining" Christ (v. 8) or "being found in Christ" (v. 9).

Paul had come to know Christ when he heard his voice on the way to Damascus, calling him from a life of sin to fellowship with him, and appointing him to be his witness in the Greco-Roman world. But the desire to be even more closely identified with Christ seems to have grown stronger as the years went by. There is nothing like this in other religions, in which there is no personal relationship with the founders of these non-Christian faiths. But Christianity is based on the person of Christ and his saving work. And since this Christ did not remain in the grave but is highly exalted today, such personal relationship is possible by the Spirit of the risen Christ.

To know Christ, writes William Barclay, is to know Christ more clearly, to love him more dearly and to follow him more nearly. Paul knew that here in this life the believer would never know Christ fully; that is something that awaits him in the world to come. However, that does not rule out the possibility of learning to know Christ more fully even now.

B. The Power

"To know him and the power of his resurrection." This seems to be simply an amplification of what it means to know Christ. One might have expected Paul to mention Christ's sufferings before he refers to his resurrection, but that is being overly finical. It may be, however, that Paul put the resurrection before the suffering since that is how he experienced Christ on the Damascus road. The risen Christ appeared to him and only after Paul became a Christian did he understand the meaning of Christ's sufferings. As a Jew he must have thought that since Christ died a shameful death on the cross, he was under a divine curse, as stated in Deuteronomy 21:23. After meeting the risen Christ, however, he realized God had reversed the judgment of the Sanhedrin and the judgment of Pilate by raising Christ from the dead. Now he could see that Christ's sufferings were part of God's salvatory plans.

What does Paul mean with "the power of his resurrection?" Is the resurrection itself the power or is Paul thinking of the power that flows from the resurrection of Christ? Surely Paul is not thinking of the power of God by which he will raise the believers from the grave when the last hour comes. Perhaps it is the power that the risen Christ exercises today, the power that flows from the risen Christ to the believer. However, it could also be that Paul is thinking of the power of God manifested in raising Christ from the dead—a power which is now active in the life of the believer. Perhaps we have a parallel in Ephesians 1:19,20: "and what is the immeasurable greatness of his power for us who believe, according to the working of his great power. God put this power to work in Christ when he raised him from the dead."

C. The Passion

"That I might know him and the power of his resurrection and the fellowship of his sufferings, becoming like him in his death." Just as the power of his resurrection amplifies what it means to know Christ personally, so also the "sharing of his sufferings."

Paul has spoken earlier of the *koinonia* (sharing, fellowship) which the Philippians had with the apostle in spreading the gospel (1:5). He also spoke of the *koinonia* of the Spirit (2:1) a fellowship of believers created by the Spirit of God. Now he speaks of the *koinonia* of Christ's sufferings. Paul wants to participate actively in Christ's sufferings.

But what kind of sufferings of Christ does Paul have in mind? Is he thinking of Christ's sufferings on the cross? In that case Paul is saying he wants to participate in the benefits of Christ's vicarious sufferings on the cross. More likely, however, he means the sufferings he himself is called upon to endure for the sake of Christ. It is through these sufferings that we enter the kingdom of God (Acts 14:22). Suffering with Christ precedes being glorified with him (Rom. 8:17). Such sufferings, of course, are not worthy to be compared with the glory that is to be revealed (Rom. 8:18). Sufferings for Christ would, in the case of Paul, include such things as imprisonment, flogging, hardships and privations, including mental anguish (2 Cor. 11:23-28). It is in the midst of such sufferings that Paul experiences the power of the risen Christ.

That these sufferings are not unrelated to Christ's death on the cross can be seen from the expression "being conformed to his death." The verb "conformed" occurs nowhere else in the Greek Bible, although the noun does (see 3:21). To be conformed to Christ's death is similar to being "crucified with Christ" (Gal. 2:19). But how are we to understand this? Perhaps there is more than one aspect to consider. Paul wanted to be identified with the crucified Christ by laying down his life; he wanted to be identified with Christ's sufferings in daily life; he wanted to experience his incorporation into Christ at a deeper level.

To be conformed to Christ in his death could be seen as pointing to martyrdom. That Paul saw his imprisonment as possibly ending in death can be seen from other passages in Philippians (e.g., 2:17). There came a time in the early church when Christians longed for a martyr's death. The outstanding example from the beginning of the second century is Ignatius, the bishop of Antioch. As he was taken to Rome where he was to be put to death, he wrote to the Roman church, to do nothing to obtain his release. He was looking forward to dying for his Lord. This somewhat morbid attitude is not reflected in Paul's letters. Paul is glad to be alive and in fact would like to remain so and serve Christ (see 1:24,25). If, however, in the mysterious wisdom of God he should have to die, he is ready for that too (see 1:20). It is doubtful then that to be conformed to Christ's death means simply to die a martyr's death.

Another way of reading our text is to see the sufferings which Paul had to endure in his apostolic ministry as similar to those which Jesus endured in his earthly life. To the Colossians he writes he is completing "what is lacking in Christ's afflications for the sake of his body, the church" (1:24). Paul could claim that he bore the marks of the Lord Jesus in his body (Gal. 6:17). The participle "being conformed" suggests ongoing action, a process, and so one might ask the question whether Paul's earlier sufferings were more like Christ's than those which he endured later. So perhaps there is even another way of reading our text!

Being conformed to Christ in his death is obviously metaphorical language. Paul wants to be completely identified with his Lord and he is confident that God is using his sufferings for Christ's cause to make him more Christlike. By the Spirit of God the difficulties and tragedies of Paul's life become the means by which Paul's character is transformed into the image of Christ. Paul frequently speaks of dying and rising with Christ (e.g., Rom. 6:4-6). Here he mentions only the dying, but in the next verse we have a reference to the rising. The Christian life is attended by much suffering but God uses these trials to transform us from one glory to another (2 Cor. 3:18).

III. HIS EXPECTATION FOR THE FUTURE (v. 11)

"If somehow I may attain the resurrection from the dead." Whereas being conformed to Christ's death is an ongoing process, the resurrection of which Paul speaks in this verse is a future event. Although dying and rising with Christ are two aspects of the believer's present life, here the two are seen as separate in time. One might think of the resurrection as the goal toward which the conforming process is pointing and moving. He has already stated his desire to experience the power of Christ's resurrection in this life, but there is a resurrection of the body which occurs at Christ's parousia, and Paul looks forward to that event with great expectation.

The hope of the resurrection is expressed in our verse in a rather unusual way: "if, perhaps, somehow." It almost appears as if Paul is doubtful of his future resurrection and he is making the hope of the resurrection somewhat contingent on his being conformed to Christ's death. However, one can also read Paul's words as the language of expectation; he has not attained to the resurrection, has not yet participated in it, and so he cannot write as if he had already reached that goal. In 1:23 he expresses complete confidence that he will go to be with Christ when he dies.

Some scholars suggest that Paul's tenuous language is simply an expression of his humility. He knows he cannot attain to that glorious goal in his own strength. Others claim that while Paul has no doubts about the goal, namely the resurrection of the body, he does not yet know by which route God will take him there. "In some way" he will attain to that goal, but it could be by martyrdom or some other way. In fact, he might even be alive at Christ's coming. His resurrection is a certainty, but what lies between the present and that great event is unknown to the apostle. He has tasted the powers of the age to come, the power of the resurrection (v. 10), but he is still in the present age. And in this present age the process of being transformed into Christ's image goes on. This process will be complete only when the resurrection takes place.

Paul uses somewhat unusual language to speak of the resurrection at this point. The word *exanastasis* (out-resurrection) occurs nowhere else in the Greek Bible. Literally it means "out from among the dead ones." This has led some Bible readers to see something else here than the resurrection at the end of the age when Christ appears in glory. Some have suggested a special resurrection for the martyrs but there is no reason to hold such a view. Others have thought of it as a resurrection directly after death, but that is also not in keeping with New Testament teaching. Still others have divided Christ's coming into two and connect the "out-resurrection" with the first coming, the Rapture. But there are no grounds for dividing Christ's coming in this way. The resurrection takes place at the parousia. To be sure, John (in Revelation 20) speaks of a first resurrection (that of the saints) and also the resurrection of evildoers, but that distinction is not a focus in our text. Therefore we should not make the compound, "out-resurrection" refer to anything other than the resurrection of the body when Christ returns.

Review Questions

1. What happened in Paul's life that completely upset his value system?

2. *Did Paul as a Christian despise his Jewish heritage?*

3. *What does it mean "to know Christ?"*

4. *What did Paul mean by his "own righteousness?"*

5. *How does the "righteousness from God" differ from self-righteousness?*

6. *How can a believer experience the "power of Christ's resurrection?"*

7. *What might "the fellowship of his sufferings" mean for us who live in a land of freedom?*

8. *What is the difference between being raised with Christ now (see Col. 3:1) and the resurrection for which Paul hopes in verse 11?*

CHAPTER ELEVEN

Already But Not Yet (3:12-21)

Not that I have already obtained this or have already reached the goal; but I press on to make it my own, because Christ Jesus has made me his own. Beloved, I do not consider that I have made it my own; but this one thing I do: forgetting what lies behind and straining forward to what lies ahead, I press on toward the goal for the prize of the heavenly call of God in Christ Jesus. Let those of us then who are mature be of the same mind; and if you think differently about anything, this too God will reveal to you. Only let us hold fast to what we have attained. Brothers and sisters, join in imitating me, and observe those who live according to the example you have in us. For many live as enemies of the cross of Christ; I have often told you of them, and now I tell you even with tears. Their end is destruction; their god is the belly; and their glory is in their shame; their minds are set on earthly things. But our citizenship is in heaven, and it is from there that we are expecting a Savior, the Lord Jesus Christ. He will transform the body of our humiliation that it may be conformed to the body of his glory, by the power that also enables him to make all things subject to himself (Philippians 3:12-21).

In the preceding passage (vv. 8-11) Paul makes the claim that his desire to know Christ is the all consuming passion of his life. The Philippians would have no trouble believing him. No doubt they had long been impressed with Paul's commitment to Christ and his kingdom. But Paul was unique. He was an apostle; he had a divine calling. Surely he could not expect ordinary Christians in Philippi to follow his example! For the apostle to have attained such dazzling heights of Christian perfection was one thing, but for the readers to attain to perfection was quite another matter.

Paul must have anticipated such thoughts and seeks to correct any possible misunderstandings about Christian perfection. He confesses humbly that he too is far from perfect and that he is still on the way; he has not yet reached the goal. Although he has counted all things as loss for the sake of Christ, he has not yet attained to perfection. He did not experience all there is to the Christian life in one grand sweep on the Damascus Road.

Chuck Colson, the converted Watergate criminal, wrote after a few years of Christian experience about the "perplexing mysteries of the Christian life:" "The deeper one's commitment and the longer one struggles to follow Christ, the more distance one realizes there is to travel. A true disciple, though experiencing a deepening communion with Christ, may at the same time become increasingly sensitive to his own shortcomings even to the point of questioning the validity of his own conversion" (Life Sentence, p. 274). How true! There is always something in our lives that seems unfinished; we are sculptures with some pieces missing. We feel keenly, as Paul describes it in this passage, that there is an "already," but there is also a "not yet." Let us listen to the apostle as he writes about this tension in the Christian life.

I. PRESSING ON TOWARD THE GOAL (vv. 12-16)

A. The Humble Affirmation (vv. 12a,13a)

"Not that I have already obtained this or have already reached the goal . . . Beloved, I do not consider that I have made it my own." Here we have an emphatic disclaimer: "Not that I have already obtained." He does not say what it is he has not yet obtained. Is it the prize at the end of the race (v. 14)? Is he thinking of the resurrection of the body (v. 11)? Does he have moral and spiritual perfection in mind? Or does he mean he does not yet know Christ as fully as he would like? Perhaps the following phrase, "or have already been perfected," answers our question. Paul is not yet perfect.

The verb *teleioo* (to perfect) has a range of meanings: to complete, finish, accomplish, bring something to an end. Very likely Paul knew of people who claimed perfection. That Paul had not yet reached eschatological perfection is clear, for he is still at home in the body and away from the Lord. However, he seems to have moral or spiritual perfection in mind. This too he has not yet obtained.

In verse 13 he repeats the disclaimer made in verse 12: "Brothers, I do not consider myself to have grasped it." Some early manuscripts have "not yet" instead of the simple "not," but that is probably a correction made by some scribe(s) who saw that "not yet" was implied in Paul's statement. He addresses his readers as "brothers," not only to remind them of his affection for them but also to arrest their attention, for what he has to say is very important.

The apostle has not yet attained to the full knowledge of Christ, nor has he already grasped the prize that awaits him at the end of the race, nor has he attained to moral perfection. Believers, however, face another danger: to be satisfied with imperfection. And lest any of his readers fall into that trap, Paul will describe his aspirations in spite of or because of his imperfections.

B. Fervent Aspiration (vv. 12b,13b)

"But I press on to make it my own, because Christ Jesus has made me his own . . . but this one thing I do: forgetting what lies behind and straining forward to what lies ahead ...." The verb "press on" (*dioko*) figuratively describes Paul's zealous pursuit of perfection. The present tense suggests this is an ongoing pursuit of a goal that is not yet within his grasp. But he wants to lay hold of it. Having discovered the grace of God at such a profound level, Paul could have simply reveled in his conversion experience and waited for the parousia to happen. But no, he had to press on. Why?

1. The Spiritual Motive. "Because I was grasped by Christ." We take the prepositional phrase "for which" to have a causal meaning. The reference no doubt is to his experience on the way to Damascus when Christ "grasped" the fiery persecutor, dashed him to the ground, blinded him with the light from heaven, and then led him out of darkness into the marvelous light of the knowledge of Christ. Paul was captured by Christ and the rest of his life was but a footnote to that encounter. When Christ laid hold of him on that memorable day before the gates of Damascus, he put a deep desire into Paul's heart: to become more like his Master and finally to arrive at perfection in the presence of God.

    2. The Potential Obstacle. "Forgetting the things behind." The style here is staccato, abrupt. "One thing . . . forgetting the things behind." We have to add a verb to complete the interjection "one thing." Perhaps "all I can say is this" (NEB) is an appropriate rendering, or "my one thought is this." The picture seems to be that of a runner who will let nothing deter him from arriving at the goal. To look back over his shoulder at the competitors would hinder a runner in his race. Nor would it help a runner if he or she constantly looked back to see how much ground they had already covered.

    Similarly Paul continuously ("forgetting" is in the present tense) forgets the things behind. What are the things behind which he forgets? We know he never forgot his sinful past, for he refers to it repeatedly. However, because God had forgiven his past, the memory of it serves as a means of grace rather than a heavy burden of guilt. Does he mean his past advantages and privileges which he mentioned in verses 5 and 6? Hardly, for he recalls them with the caveat that he has given them up for the sake of Christ. Perhaps the forgetting that Paul has in mind refers to his accomplishments as a Christian believer, as an apostle. Pride in one's attainments can become a serious obstacle in running the race of faith. Upon occasion Paul does recall his past missionary accomplishments (cf. I Cor. 15:10) but not in order to rest on his laurels or to nurture feelings of self-satisfaction.

    3. The Practical Expression. "Straining forward to what lies ahead." A runner not only avoids looking back constantly, he must also strain forward with all his or her might if the goal is to be reached. The verb "to strain forward" is taken from the arena and pictures the Christian as a runner with his body bent over, his hand outstretched, his head fixed forward, and his eye fastened on the goal. It underscores the intensity of the apostle's desire to achieve the hoped-for goal, namely, full and complete perfection.

Straining forward in the Christian race must, of course, not be literalized to the point where progress is measured in terms of physical exertion. When L.E. Maxwell, founder of Prairie Bible Institute, of whom I have fond memories from student days, came to know Christ, he was mortified to discover there was still sin left in his life. He had spent his teenage years in a pool hall his father owned in Kansas City, but by God's grace was delivered from his past life of sin. However, when he found that conversion had not made him perfect, he spent weeks trying to find the golden key that would unlock the gates of perfection. He lost fifteen pounds in the effort, only to discover that sinlessness is not something the believer can attain to this side of heaven. Also to strain forward does not mean we take our spiritual temperature daily to see whether we have made progress or not. We cannot measure spiritual growth as one measures the physical growth of a child with a yardstick. We have the deep satisfaction of having been accepted just as we are into the family of God; at the same time there remains a deep longing to be transformed into the image of Christ., Missionary writer E. Stanley Jones suggested we should look upon ourselves neither as "worm" or "wonder," but rather as "a bundle of possibilities in Christ." That would probably be an accurate description of Paul's aspirations.

C. The Constant Stimulation (v. 14)

"I press on toward the goal for the prize of the heavenly call of God in Christ Jesus." The athletic figure of speech is drawn out further: Paul sees himself as a runner who has his eye on the prize, and this prospect stimulates him in his race. He is running straight towards the goal in order to win the prize. Although the verb "pursue" (*dioko,* as in v. 12) need not mean to run in a race, the words "goal" (*skopos*—only here in the New Testament) and "prize" (*brabeion*) come from the world of athletics. Paul then is not running aimlessly; he is heading straight for the goal. Nothing is permitted to distract him, for at the end of the race the prize awaits him.

The language here resembles I Corinthians 9:24 where Paul points out that many runners take part, but only one wins the prize. The notion of coming first in the race is, however, not part of the metaphor, for the same reward is given to all who finish the Christian race. Paul makes this clear in 2 Timothy 4:8 where he speaks of the victory wreath that he will be awarded by the righteous Judge, but then adds "and to all who have longed for his appearing."

But what is the prize Paul is looking for? The answer is "the upward calling of God in Christ Jesus." Does he mean that God's call to eternal life in heaven is the prize? Or is Paul simply continuing the athletic imagery in the sense that the presiding judge at the games calls the successful athletes to come and receive the prize? Perhaps it is best to understand the word "call" in its usual sense as God's call to salvation. That would mean that God has taken the initiative. He has called Paul by the gospel, and he keeps on calling him into his kingdom and his glory (I Thess. 2:12). And the prize handed out by God at the end of the race is the complete fulfillment of Paul's desire to be wholly conformed to Christ for whose sake he had given up everything. And of course Paul wants his readers to follow his example.

D. The Apostolic Exhortation (vv. 15,16)
"Let those of us then who are mature be of the same mind; and if you think differently about anything, this too God will reveal to you. Only let us hold fast to what we have attained."
1. To Maturity (v. 15a). Paul now invites his readers to share his aspirations with him. He has admitted he is not yet perfect, but he is on the way to that final goal which promises perfection in the presence of God. What then does he mean when he says, "let those of us who are 'perfect' have this mind?" Is this irony or a sincere conviction of Paul? How can he include himself among the "perfect" when he has just confessed that he is still imperfect?

The word "perfect" (*teleios*) should probably be understood in the sense of "mature." This word is frequently found in the Greek translation of the Old Testament, rendering the Hebrew *tamim*, which has the meaning of wholeness. A person who is faithful to God is said to be perfect. Members of the Qumran community also were called "perfect" (IQS 8:20), in the sense that they were fulfilling God's will. Jesus also summons his followers to be perfect (Mt. 5:48), by showing kindness to all people, as God does. A person who does not offend others in words, says James, is perfect (Jam. 3:2). We suggest therefore that Paul uses the word "perfect" in the sense of mature or whole.

Perhaps an illustration would help us. When a healthy child is born, one might say it is "perfect." All the limbs are there; the digestive and respiratory systems are working normally, and so forth. However, it is not yet "perfect" in the sense that it has a long way to grow before it becomes an adult. Similarly, believers can be called "perfect" if their hearts are fully turned toward God and his will, but we all have a long way to go before we reach that perfection which awaits us when we enter the gates of glory. We recognize, of course, that there are many immature Christians, and Paul seems to suggest that possibility when he says "as many of us as are mature." And those who fall into that category are invited to share in Paul's aspirations: "Let us have this attitude." What attitude? The attitude Paul displayed by forgetting the things behind and stretching forward to the goal.

2. To Openness (v. 15b). "And if you think differently about anything, this too God will reveal to you." There will never be complete agreement among believers on all the details of the Christian life, and Paul is aware of that. However, Paul is confident that if there are inconsistencies in the faith of the readers, God will give them further light. In addition to the mature mind which many of his readers have, God will reveal other things to them. That would be a positive way of reading the text. There are scholars, on the other hand, who think Paul is offering a corrective to views held by his readers. If so, he does not tell us what these are. Perhaps it is best then to understand him to say that if they are open to receive further light from God, God is sure to give it to them.

3. To Consistency (v. 16). "Only let us hold fast to what we have attained." "To hold fast" translates the Greek verb *stoicheo*, which means to walk in a straight line, to march in step, stand in line, agree, follow, to line up. It is also found in Galatians 6:16 where it is connected with the noun "rule" (*kanon*) and for that reason some manuscripts here also have "to walk according to this rule." The verb seems to imply some kind of standard in any case: "According to the same rules" (GNB).

The apostle is urging his readers to continue in the manner they have begun and live according to the guidelines of Christian living he had given them when they first heard the gospel. In I Corinthians 4:17 Paul speaks of "my ways in Christ Jesus that I teach in all the churches everywhere." Paul wants the whole Christian community to move forward in unity. Also he wants their everyday life to be in harmony with their mature attitude for which he commends them.

II. FOLLOWING GOOD EXAMPLES (vv. 17-19)

A. Positive Patterns (v. 17)

"Brothers and sisters, join in imitating me, and observe those who live according to the example you have in us." In everyday life human examples, patterns and heroes play an important role in determining Christian behavior. Christian ethical teachings are embodied not merely in written codes of precepts and maxims, covering every possible contingency of life, but are preeminent in the life of Jesus and his faithful followers. Paul has already given his readers models to imitate: Christ (2:5-11), Timothy and Epaphroditus. But there are others, including himself, who can model the Christian life for them.

"Brothers, be united in imitating me." Again he addresses his readers affectionately and calls upon them to be "fellow imitators" (*summimetai*) . This is the only occurrence of this word in the New Testament, although the simple *mimetes* (imitator) is found fairly frequently. The preposition *sun* (together) suggests that Paul wants the Philippians to be united in imitating him and others. But in what respect are they to imitate Paul and other mature Christians?

That Paul was careful in the way he lived so he would not be a stumbling block to others is well known (cf. I Cor. 10:32). The context here may suggest he wanted his readers to imitate him in pursuing the heavenly goal of Christlikeness. To accuse Paul of immodesty when he asks his readers to imitate him is a misdirected approach. In I Corinthians 11:1, where he calls on his readers to follow his example, he adds, "as I imitate Christ." Christ remains the supreme example to imitate, even for Paul. We should remember that in this early period of Christianity, before churches had the New Testament, the living example of those who had brought them the gospel was extremely significant.

But Paul is not the only pattern for the life of his readers. There are others, and he encourages them to pay careful attention to those who live according to the pattern which the apostles gave them. They are to notice, to keep their eyes on those whose behavior resembles that of Paul and others. The word "example" (*tupos*) is derived from the verb "to strike" and originally referred to the impress made by a blow. It then takes on the meaning of "pattern," "mold" or "type." The change from the singular ("imitate me") to the plural "us" makes it clear that Paul knows of others in the Philippian church who can serve the congregation as models for the Christian life. This was all the more important in light of the fact that there were false teachers who were attempting to pervert the apostolic gospel and whose lives did not measure up to the apostolic ideal.

B. Negative Models (vv. 18,19)

"For many live as enemies of the cross of Christ; I have often told you of them, and now I tell you even with tears. Their end is destruction; their god is the belly; and their glory is in their shame; their minds are set on earthly things." Paul has held himself and other faithful Christians up as examples because there are many people whose lives stand in opposition to the teachings of Jesus and the apostles, and they are a danger to the Philippian church. Paul had warned his readers against such people repeatedly, but now he writes to them with tears. Just who these people were is not stated, but from the description of their way of life we can gather they were people who were acquainted with the gospel. However, they seemingly had no desire to walk the Christian way. And just as Paul had great pain and anguish for his fellow countrymen (Rom. 9:1-5), so he weeps for these people. Among them may have been former converts. The apostle cries when he thinks of where they are going.

What was their guilt? "They are enemies of the cross of Christ." Were these so-called Christians under the influence of Gnosticism? Were they apostate believers? Were they Christians who just could not shake off the immoral practices of their pagan past? Perhaps it is best to see them as Christians who had a wrong understanding of grace (so F.F. Bruce). Paul knew of people who thought the more they sinned, the more God's grace would be manifested in their lives (Rom. 6:1). Paul certainly knew who these people were and so did his readers. They were probably not (or no longer) members of the church but still claimed to be Christians.

Did they not believe in the gospel in which the cross is central? They probably held to the message of the cross but denied the implications of Christ's death for daily living. By the way they lived, they made a mockery of the message of the cross. When people who claim to believe in Christ and in his saving death choose to live immoral lives, they can be described as enemies of the cross.

The apostle proceeds to speak of the awful destiny of such people. "Their end is destruction." The Greek word *telos* is used in the sense of goal or end. Obviously destruction is not their desired or intended goal, but it is the inevitable end of those who continue to live in sin. Clearly the judgment at the end of the age is in view here. Eternal destruction awaits the enemies of the cross.

Having stated the tragic outcome of their lives, Paul mentions several aspects of their behavior. "Their god is the belly." It is not quite clear what is meant by this concise statement. Some scholars have suggested that Paul had the Judaizers in mind who were constantly concerned about food laws. We would then have to read a bit of irony in Paul's description. On the other hand (and most scholars lean in this direction), Paul may have had gluttons in mind, people who were chiefly interested in the pleasures of the table. There are also those who take "belly" (*koilia* means "hollow" and is used for stomach, womb or inner person) to mean "bodily desires" of all kinds, and the word "belly" should be understood in the same sense as the word "flesh" when it is used in its ethical sense.

"Their glory is in their shame." This is an oxymoron. They are proud of what they should be ashamed. "Glory" must be understood in the context as boasting. Their way of life is shameful because of its excesses and its immoralities. And yet they rejoice in this freedom to live according to their sinful desires. Another way of reading the text is to read "shame" as a reference to circumcision in which the Judaizers boasted. However, it would be strange for Paul to speak of a "shameful member" of the body. Another view is to take shame to be a reference to the final judgment when they will be disgraced. John warns his readers to live in such a way that they need not be put to shame at Christ's coming (I Jn. 2:28). Most likely Paul has a shameful way of life in mind. Jude mentions libertines whom he compares to "wild waves of the sea with their shameful deeds showing up like foam" (Jude 13).

"They mind earthly things." They are completely oriented to this earth. "Earthly things" (*epigeia*) are temporal, transient and stand in contrast to that which is eternal and permanent, namely heavenly things (Col. 3:1). One is reminded of John Bunyan's description of the man with the muckrake, too occupied with the transient things of life to see the crown offered by God. "Earthly things" must be understood here as representing evil desires and values. There is a legitimate minding of earthly things. Believers too have duties here on earth—as husbands, wives, children, laborers and managers. Here, however, the entire orientation of people's lives is directed to the ephemeral and sinful; they "lick the earth," to use an expression from Malcolm Muggeridge. As such they stand in vivid contrast to those whose commonwealth is in heaven.

III. WAITING FOR THE SAVIOR (vv. 20,21)

"But our citizenship is in heaven, and it is from there that we are expecting a Savior, the Lord Jesus Christ. He will transform the body of our humiliation that it may be conformed to the body of his glory, by the power that also enables him to make all things subject to himself."

A. The Expectation (v. 20)

After the digression in verses 18 and 19 in which Paul warns the readers against those who have perverted the Christian way of life, he describes the genuine believers. In contrast to those whose minds are focused on the earth are those whose *politeuma* (citizenship) is in heaven. *Politeuma* is found only here in the New Testament and means "commonwealth," "citizenship," "colony" or "state." Since Philippi had received special privileges at the hand of Rome, it was treated as if it were on Italian soil; it was a little "Rome" in Macedonia. Similarly, believers in Philippi (and other cities of this world) live here on earth, but they belong to a country for which the saints are waiting; a country in which they hold citizenship and it is according to those laws they seek to order their lives.

And since the true capital city of the believer is the "Jerusalem that is above" (Gal. 4:26), they naturally expect their Savior to come some day and bring them home to glory. They "eagerly wait" (*apekdechomai* is a double compound) for the Deliverer (*Soter* means Deliverer, Savior). The deliverance Paul has in mind is that which occurs at the end of the age; it is final deliverance, ultimate salvation. In I Thessalonians 1:10 Paul uses similar language: "To wait for his Son from heaven . . . Jesus, who rescues us from the wrath that is coming." Although God is also called Savior in the Scriptures, here clearly the Savior is Jesus Christ the Lord. Although Paul includes himself among the "we" who wait for the Savior, it would be pressing the language too far if, on the basis of this verse, we should infer that Paul was certain he would still be alive when Christ returned. He can also say "whether we live or die" (cf. I Thess. 5:10). This is the language of faith. Believers in every generation wait for the Savior to come, but they also know that with the Lord a thousand years are like one day.

To wait for the Savior does not mean Christians constantly think about Christ's return or always make that the subject of their conversation. Rather, they order their lives and priorities in such a way that they are ready when the bridegroom comes. In the anonymous Letter to Diognetus, a second century letter, we read about early Christians: "Although they live in Greek and barbarian cities alike, as each man's lot has been cast, and follow the customs of the country in clothing and food and other matters of daily living, at the same time they give proof of the remarkable and admittedly extraordinary constitution of their own commonwealth. They live in their own countries, but only as aliens. They have a share in everything as citizens and endure everything as foreigners. Every foreign land is their fatherland and every fatherland is their homeland" (5:4).

B. Transformation (v. 21)

Paul singles out one particular aspect of Christ's coming to deliver us at the end of the age: he will transform the body of our humiliation. In Romans 8:23 Paul calls this "the redemption of our bodies."

In order to enter God's eternal kingdom we have to be transformed, for flesh and blood cannot inherit that coming kingdom (I Cor. 15:51-58). Not only will the dead be raised when Christ appears, but the living will be given new bodies.

"The body of humiliation" is a reference to "our weak mortal bodies" (GNB) but it includes our whole personality. The rendering of the KJV ("vile body") can easily be misconstrued to suggest that Paul had a negative view of the human body. Nowhere does Paul speak pejoratively of the human body. It is God's creation. But because of our fallenness, our mortality, our weakness, it can be called a body representing a state of humiliation.

When Christ appears he will transform our bodies so they conform to his glorious body. The bodies we will possess in the heavenly state will be like Christ's body. That means our bodies will be glorious, strong, imperishable and "spiritual" (I Cor. 15:38-49). They will be in every respect suited to the heavenly existence that awaits the believer.

Paul has good reason to hope for such a transformation, for Christ will carry out this final act of deliverance "according to the effective working (*energeia*) of the one who enables him to subject all things to himself." *Energeia* always denotes supernatural power, and usually divine power (in a few instances, Satanic power). Christ is able to subject the whole universe to himself and so he surely is able to transform our bodies to his own likeness.

Review Questions

1. Is Christian perfection, in the sense of sinlessness, attainable in this life?

2. Does this mean we must remain content with our sinful ways?

3. What kind of things should we "forget" and what are the things we should "remember" in our Christian life?

4. In what sense can believers be said to be "perfect" (v. 15) even now?

5. *How has your life been affected by good examples in the Christian community?*

6. *What does it mean to be "earthly minded?"*

7. *How does the conviction that we are citizens of a heavenly commonwealth make a difference in our everyday life?*

8. *What kind of bodies will we have when we pass through the gates of glory?*

CHAPTER TWELVE

ENCOURAGING ADMONITIONS (4:1-9)

Therefore, my brothers and sisters, whom I love and long for, my joy and crown, stand firm in the Lord in this way, my beloved. I urge Euodia and I urge Syntyche to be of the same mind in the Lord. Yes, and I ask you also, my loyal companion, help these women, for they have struggled beside me in the work of the gospel, together with Clement and the rest of my coworkers , whose names are in the book of life. Rejoice in the Lord always; again I will say, Rejoice. Let your gentleness be known to everyone. The Lord is near. Do not worry about anything, but in everything by prayer and supplication with thanksgiving let your requests be made known to God. And the peace of God, which surpasses all understanding, will guard your hearts and your minds in Christ Jesus. Finally, beloved, whatever is true, whatever is honorable, whatever is just, whatever is pure, whatever is pleasing, whatever is commendable, if there is any excellence and if there is anything worthy of praise, think about these things. Keep on doing the things that you have learned and received and heard and seen in me, and the God of peace will be with you (Philippians 4:1-9).

There were no chapter divisions in Paul's letter to the Philippians. They were added much later and although they are convenient for locating passages, they tend to break up Paul's train of thought. In fact, in the case of our text, we are not sure whether 4:1 begins a new chapter or whether it is the conclusion of chapter 3.

In any case, the words "so then" connect our passage closely with what has gone on before. The apostle has just warned his readers against those who have become the enemies of the cross and that leads him to stress the importance of steadfastness in the Christian faith. This is, however, not the first time in this short epistle that Paul has underscored the need for firmness. In fact, it seems as he brings the letter to a close he picks up several themes he has touched upon earlier.

The passage opens with five terms of endearment. He addresses his readers in very affectionate terms, unparalleled in any other letter. These tender words are not simply sentimental outbursts, but show the deep and strong regard of the apostle for his readers. Also, they help to establish rapport between apostle and readers and will make it easier for them to receive his encouraging admonitions.

I. THE ADMONITION TO STEADFASTNESS (v. 1)

"Therefore, my brothers and sisters, whom I love and long for, my joy and crown, stand firm in the Lord in this way, my beloved." Once again he addresses them as his brothers and sisters (see 1:12; 3:1,13,17). Paul teaches elsewhere (e.g., Eph. 2:19) that the church is a family. All believers belong to the same household; all call upon the same Father; all confess the same Lord.

The word "beloved" (*agapetoi*) occurs twice in this verse and shows the warmth of Paul's affection for the Philippians. The verbal adjective "longed for" occurs nowhere else in the New Testament. However, a cognate verb (*epipotheo*) is found in 1:8 where Paul expresses his longing for his readers, and in 2:26 it describes the anxiety of Epaphroditus for his home church. "Longed for" expresses the pain Paul feels in his heart because of his forced separation from the readers. When one considers how studiously a Pharisee would try to keep separate from all Gentiles lest he defile himself, we cannot help but marvel at the miracle of God's grace in the life of Paul. Now he longs for the Philippian believers, most of whom were Gentiles.

The pain of separation is, however, mixed with joy as he thinks of his readers. They are the source and the cause of his joy. It need not be reiterated that joy is one of the main themes of this letter. There is a parallel to our text in I Thessalonians 2:19 where the Thessalonians are said to be Paul's "joy and crown" on the day of Christ's return. This has led some readers to interpret "joy and crown" in our passage as pointing to the future when Paul, together with his readers will stand before the throne of God. However, it is best to understand the apostle as saying the Philippians are a source of joy for him in the present.

Finally, he calls them "his crown." The word *stephanos* is not the royal diadem, nor does it necessarily refer to the crown given to the believer at the last day. *Stephanos* is a garland placed on the head of a guest at a banquet or a wreath given to a victor. One might say then the Philippians are the cause of festal joy for Paul; he is proud of them. Of course, we should not rule out the future dimension of the Christian life. The Philippians will also be a crown on Paul's head at Christ's parousia; they will be an honor to him.

After listening to this fivefold affectionate address, it may be inferred that the dangers Paul had spoken about in chapter 3 had not yet made appreciable inroads in the church. By and large they have remained faithful to Christ. However, all believers are subject to attacks by the evil one and so once again Paul admonishes them to stand firm.

The command to stand firm is linked with an adverb ("thus" or "so") that suggests a certain manner of standing fast. Does he mean they are to stand firm the way Paul stands firm (cf. 3:17) or as it is fitting for members of the heavenly commonwealth (3:20,21) who are waiting for the Savior to return? In 1:27 the call to firmness is given in view of the attacks of adversaries. Here no adversaries are mentioned but there are dangers lurking along the Christian way and the readers are asked to stand firm as a soldier in battle.

Fortunately they are not left to their own resources when it comes to steadfastness. Paul appeals to them to stand fast "in the Lord." Implied in that phrase is they can be strong only in fellowship with

Christ. Also, the Lord has promised to keep his own safe. Perhaps "in the Lord" also suggests they must stand firm in obedience to the Lord.

We are living in days of compromise. It is not popular today to hold convictions about anything, especially not religious truths and values. Certitude about biblical teachings is frowned upon in our society. Of course, firmness must not be confused with stubbornness or the unwillingness to make changes in matters that are not fundamental to our Christian life. However, when it comes to the basic apostolic doctrines and fundamental ethical principles, we dare not compromise, lest we be swept away. Paul writes in a similar vein to the Ephesians: "Therefore, take up the whole armor of God, so that you may be able to withstand on that evil day, and having done everything, to stand firm, stand therefore" (6:13).

II. THE ADMONITION TO UNANIMITY (vv. 2,3)

"I urge Euodia and I urge Syntyche to be of the same mind in the Lord. Yes, and I ask you also, my loyal companion, help these women, for they have struggled beside me in the work of the gospel, together with Clement and the rest of my coworkers, whose names are in the book of life."

A. The Problem (v. 2)

In his direct personal appeal for unity, Paul mentions two women by name. The verb *parakaleo* has a wide range of meanings: to summon, exhort, urge, comfort, encourage and so forth. Here the verb means to beg, to appeal, to exhort. If Paul had used the verb once, the appeal would have been strong enough, but he repeats it: "I exhort Euodia and I exhort Syntyche."

Unfortunately we know nothing about these women. The names are not uncommon in Greek. Etymologically Euodia means "a good journey" and Syntyche "happy chance, luck," but we should not make anything of these etymologies. These women evidently were active members of the church and their disagreements threatened the unity of the congregation. Had their disagreements not been public knowledge, Paul would certainly not have mentioned them by name.

The attempt to identify one of them with Lydia, who is known to us from the book of Acts as the first convert in Philippi (Acts 16:14ff.), leads nowhere. Nor can we take seriously the suggestion that the two names are used allegorically to represent the Jewish and Gentile factions in the church. One of the early church Fathers thought Syntyche should be spelled Syntyches and Paul had the Philippian jailor in mind and not a woman. But no amount of speculation will help us to identify these women.

Paul urges these women to be of the same mind. That is precisely what he earlier asked all Christians to be (2:2). The apostle does not expect Christians to think alike about all matters, but there was something wrong with the attitudes of these two women. They are to have the same mind "in the Lord," i.e., as befits people who are in fellowship with Christ and in submission to him. The fact that only two women are singled out suggests they were very influential. Perhaps they were charter members, deaconesses or leaders of house churches.

B. The Resolution (v. 3a)
"Yes, I ask you also, my loyal companion, help these women." It appears as if the two women in question could not come together on their own; they needed a third party to help them. And so he asks one of his coworkers to give them a hand. Who this "genuine yoke-fellow" was is not known, but evidently the church would know who was meant. Attempts at identifying this unknown coworker abound. Clement of Alexandria thought Paul was addressing his own wife, but we don't know Paul as a married man. Others have suggested Lydia, Timothy, Silas, Epaphroditus (who was carrying the letter), Luke or the bishop of the church. Another way of identifying this coworker is to take the word Zyzygos (yoke-fellow) to be a proper noun, the name of a person. But all this is speculative. Whoever this genuine yoke-fellow was, Paul is asking him to help these two women to be reconciled.

C. The Recognition (v. 3b)
"For they have struggled beside me in the work of the gospel, together with Clement and the rest of my coworkers, whose names

are in the book of life." Paul pays high tribute to these women and he uses an athletic metaphor to indicate their efforts in furthering the cause of Christ. *Sunathleo* (to play the game together) is used here for the second time in this letter (see 1:27). It has come to mean to contend or to struggle along with. They participated with Paul in the suffering that usually attended the spread of the gospel in the early period of the Christian church. Perhaps they played an important role when the Philippian church was founded but we really know nothing definite about their ministry. Paul had formerly persecuted both men and women, and from that one can gather he saw in Christian women a force to be reckoned with.

With Euodia and Syntyche Paul points to Clement and the rest of his fellow-workers whose names are in the book of life. Just who this Clement was we do not know, but he must have been well known in the Philippian church and so Paul does not need to identify him more precisely. It was a common Roman name. But, having mentioned three people by name, it occurs to Paul there was really a host of others who had worked with him in the cause of the kingdom of God, and so he includes "the rest of my fellow-workers."

They had names too but they were too numerous to be mentioned. Fortunately their names are all recorded in the book of life. This is an expression as old as the early pages of the Bible (Ex. 32:32). Jesus assured his disciples that "their names are written in heaven" (Lk. 10:20). And the fearless confessors in the book of Revelation (3:5) have the promise that their names will not be removed from the book of life. In the end all those not written in the book of life will be cast into the lake of fire (Rev. 20:11f.). To have one's name written in the book of life means that one belongs to God; it also means that one has eternal life.

III. ADMONITION TO CHRISTIAN VIRTUES (vv. 4-9)

A. Joyfulness (v. 4)

"Rejoice in the Lord always; again I will say, Rejoice." Since the verb *chairein* (rejoice) is used also as a parting greeting, some think Paul really means "farewell," but that is hardly fitting here. Goodspeed, for example, has "Good-bye, and the Lord be with you always; again I say, Good-bye." The word "always" would seem to rule out the meaning of "farewell." We have a parallel in I Thessalonians 5:16, "Rejoice always."

Chapter 3 began with "Rejoice in the Lord" and now he will say it again. It is one of the fundamental themes of this letter. The joy Paul has in mind is independent of circumstances. Paul himself is in prison and he knows his readers also have trials to face because of their faith. The source of Christian joy is "in the Lord." It is that deep assurance which the believer has in his or her heart that regardless of difficulties the Christian life might bring, God is leading his children to glory. It is, one might say, "eschatological" joy. Perhaps the reference to the book of life (v. 3) reminded Paul of the words of Jesus to his disciples to rejoice because their names were written in the book of life (Lk. 10:20). Joy is a fundamental characteristic of the kingdom of God (Rom. 14:17).

B. Gentleness (v. 5)

"Let your gentleness be known to everyone. The Lord is near." Gentleness (*epieikes*), like joy, is a fruit of the Spirit (Gal. 5:22). Tyndale rendered this word "softness," the Douay-Rheims has "modesty," English Revised Version has "forbearance" and the AV has "moderation." In the New Testament it is Christ who serves the believer as the model in this particular virtue. In 2 Corinthians 10:1 Paul mentions the "meekness and gentleness of Christ." Christian ethics are Christomorphic, i.e., believers are to conform to the example set for us by our Lord.

Gentleness has to do with that patient steadfastness manifested when believers are treated unjustly, unfairly and disgracefully. Magnanimity is such an important virtue that Paul wants everyone to know it, to see it. Not only within the circle of Christian friends but in the world, "to all men," the believer is to show mellowness and courtesy, reasonableness and generosity.

And the encouragement to manifest this fruit of the Spirit in the community is given in the additional statement "The Lord is near." Whether the word "near" is to be understood spatially or temporally is not clear. If the meaning is spatial, then Paul assures his readers that Christ is always with them. He is close by; he observes how they treat others and he is there to help them live right. If, on the other hand, the word "near" points to the return of Christ at the end of the age, then it is probably an incentive to right living. It could also be an encouragement to those who patiently endure hatred and opposition from unbelievers, that when the Lord comes he will make everything right. It is possible that both meanings are found in the word "near" and then we do not have to make a decision on whether it is to be understood spatially or temporally.

C. Trustfulness (vv. 6,7)
1. The Prohibition (v. 6a). "Do not worry about anything." Literally we might say "stop worrying about anything." The verb "to worry" (*merimnao*) is onomatopoeic, meaning sound and sense agree. Paul is warning against fretfulness which betrays a lack of trust in God's care. This does not mean we do not feel pain, frustration, loss, hunger or hurt, but we can entrust ourselves into God's hands.

In Philippians 2:20 this same verb had a positive meaning for concern about the church, but here it is used pejoratively. Paul's prohibition echoes the teaching of Jesus in the Sermon on the Mount (Mt. 6:25-34), where anxiety about the things of this life is said to be typical of the pagan world (v. 32). The apostle is not making light of the troubles that beset believers in this life, but he knows that God is greater than all the trials of life.

2. The Alternative (v. 6b). "But in everything by prayer and supplication with thanksgiving let your requests be known to God." There is nothing too difficult for God's power, there is nothing too small for his concern, and there is nothing too complicated for his wisdom.

Three words are used for prayer: prayer (*proseuche*), petition (*deesis*) and request (*aitema*). The first is the more general word for prayer; the second emphasizes the element of petition or entreaty; the third is the thing that is asked for. Perhaps the three words are used synonymously at this point. Heaping up words with similar meanings for the sake of emphasis is not uncommon in Paul's letters.

All the petitions that are offered up to God are to be offered "with thanksgiving" (*eucharistia*). Jesus taught that when his children pray they can be sure their heavenly Father knows all about their needs (Mt. 6:32), and yet here Paul exhorts his readers to make their petitions known to God. By describing their needs before God his children confess they are dependent on him and they also acknowledge that he is able to help them. Whereas the ungodly refuse to give thanks to the Creator (Rom. 1:21), the believer's life is characterized by thanksgiving.

3. The Blessing (v.- 7). "And the peace of God which surpasses all understanding, will guard your hearts and minds in Christ Jesus." The peace that Paul promises his readers if they stop worrying and commit their needs to God in prayer with thanksgiving comes from God. The expression "peace of God" is unique; it occurs nowhere else in the New Testament (Col. 3:15 has "the peace of Christ"). The question is: does this refer to the peace that comes from being justified by faith (Rom. 5:1)? Does it refer to the inward peace of the soul that comes from the knowledge that one's sins are forgiven? Or does it refer to God's own serenity? God himself is not beset by anxieties as we are. Perhaps it is best to take all these meanings into account. Peace characterizes God. It is his very nature, and this peace is offered to the believer who casts his anxieties on the Lord and expresses his trust and confidence through prayer and thanksgiving.

This peace is described as surpassing all understanding. No human mind can comprehend it. Also, it accomplishes more than any human plan or scheme could possibly achieve. All our efforts to make ourselves secure in this world cannot achieve for us what the peace of God can. It is more effective in removing anxieties than any insurance policy.

This peace, says Paul, "will guard your hearts and minds in Christ Jesus." The verb *phroureo* (guard) is a military metaphor and means to stand sentry, to garrison, to guard, to preserve. Peace is personified here as doing guard duty; it will keep out anxiety and other intruders. "Hearts and minds" seem to overlap in meaning. If a distinction is made, then "hearts" would have a wider meaning, including the emotions, while "minds" would refer to the thinking processes. The two together would encompass the whole inner life of the person. God's peace will stand guard over those who are "in Christ Jesus," i.e., in fellowship with him. John Bunyan has a word picture of Mr. God's Peace in the town of Mansoul keeping watch, and the result is harmony, happiness, joy and health.

D. Noble-mindedness (vv. 8,9)

"Finally, beloved, whatever is true, whatever is honorable, whatever is just, whatever is pure, whatever is pleasing, whatever is commendable, if there is any excellence and if there is anything worthy of praise, think about these things. Keep on doing the things that you have learned and received and heard and seen in me and the God of peace will be with you."

The word "finally" (as for the rest) could suggests that Paul is drawing his letter to a close. On the other hand, the word could indicate the apostle has some additional thoughts and exhortations to add. As good food is necessary for bodily health, so good thoughts are necessary for mental and spiritual health. Paul asks his readers to fill their minds with those things that are good and deserve praise. Then more specifically, he lists six things they might think about and practice in daily life.

Whether Paul took over a current list of virtues from Greek moral philosophers or not is hard to determine with any certitude. But even if he did borrow the names of Greek virtues, he gives them a distinctly Christian meaning. On the other hand, it has been pointed out by scholars that with one exception all these virtues are mentioned in the Septuagint, Paul's Greek Old Testament. But regardless of the background of this list of virtues, Paul is not encouraging his readers to live up to some common religious ideals; he wants them to practice Christian graces. Let us look at these graces individually.

1. Whatever is True. The adjective "true" (*alethe*) is used in a comprehensive sense of all that is true over against what is false; for all that is real over against that which is apparent; for all that is genuine over against the imitative.

2. Whatever is Honorable. The word *semnos* (serious, sublime, dignified, noble) is found only here outside the Pastoral Epistles, where it occurs half a dozen times. Paul wants his readers to focus on noble things in contrast to all that is vulgar. William Barclay speaks of the "majesty of the Christian life."

3. Whatever is Right. Again the word is used in a comprehensive way to include all that is right with respect to God and his people. Paul assumes his readers have been sufficiently instructed in the things of God so they know what is right in God's eyes.

4. Whatever is Pure. The word can mean "chaste" (2 Cor. 11:2), innocent, morally upright. Again it is a comprehensive term for purity of thought, motive, action. Although the word can mean purity in sexual matters, it has a much wider circle of meaning.

5. Whatever is Lovely. Here we have an unusual word which is found only here in the New Testament (*prosphile*). It means lovely, pleasing, agreeable, amiable, attractive. It is that quality which endears one person to another. In contrast to that which calls forth resentment, this makes people attractive.

6. Whatever is Commendable. The Greek word *euphemos* gives us the English word "euphemism," which means basically to say something good or pleasant. In the active sense it refers to agreeable speech, and in the passive it means "well spoken of." It's a Christian grace seen in those who do not offend others by offensive behavior or speech.

After a series of adjectives in the plural, Paul gives a summary statement by using two nouns in the singular: "If there is any excellence and if there is anything worthy of praise, think about these things." Although these appear to be conditional clauses, Paul has no doubts about the presence of these virtues. The "if" should probably be rendered as "since."

The word *arete* (virtue, excellence, goodness) appears nowhere else in Paul's letters. It is found, however, in I Peter 2:9 and 2 Peter 1:3,5. It is a word that was sometimes used of God's excellence and his wonderful deeds. But here it is used of believers. In Hellenistic moral philosophy it was defined as the highest good in people. Paul uses it as a kind of summary term for Christian moral excellence and goodness. *Arete* is connected here with "praise," which has the meaning of "worthy of praise." Paul wants his readers to live in such a manner that their conduct will call forth praise on the part of their fellow human beings.

After this list of Christian virtues we have the exhortation "Keep on thinking on these things." When believers reflect on these attractive graces, this pondering will lead to everyday practice. Paul reminds them they had been instructed in these matters by the missionaries who founded the church, specifically by Paul himself. "Keep on doing the things that you have learned and received and heard and seen in me." Not only had he instructed them verbally but by his example they had learned how to live the Christian life in which the graces he has mentioned are manifested. To "learn" means more than to receive information; it includes a positive response, appropriation. "Received" is a verb that is used quite regularly for the reception of Christian tradition, both doctrinal and ethical. When Paul was in Philippi, the Philippians "heard" about the apostle's way of life and they "saw" it; they observed him and his fellow missionaries. The example of the apostles was extremely important in the early period of the Christian church when the books of the New Testament were not yet available. What Paul taught his converts he had learned from Christ (I Cor. 11:1) and so he is not embarrassed to hold his own life up as a pattern for them to follow.

Review Questions

1. *What is the difference between standing firm (v. 1) and plain stubbornness?*

2. *How many people in the Philippian church could you mention by name?*

3. *What assurance do we have that our names are written in the book of life (v.3)?*

4. *How should Christians "make known" their gentleness to all people (v. 5)?*

5. *How does the Christian practice of prayer affect one's anxieties?*

6. *Is there a connection between our thought life and our deportment (vv. 8,9)?*

CHAPTER THIRTEEN

PAUL'S GRATEFUL COMMENDATION (4:10-23)

I rejoice in the Lord greatly that now at last you have revived your concern for me; indeed, you were concerned for me, but had no opportunity to show it. Not that I am referring to being in need; for I have learned to be content with whatever I have. I know what it is to have little, and I know what it is to have plenty. In any and all circumstances I have learned the secret of being well-fed and of going hungry, of having plenty and of being in need. I can do all things through him who strengthens me. In any case, it was kind of you to share my distress. You Philippians indeed know that in the early days of the gospel, when I left Macedonia, no church shared with me in the matter of giving and receiving, except you alone. For even when I was in Thessalonica, you sent me help for my needs more than once. Not that I seek the gift, but I seek the profit that accumulates to your account. I have been paid in full and have more than enough; I am fully satisfied, now that I have received from Epaphroditus the gifts you sent, a fragrant offering, a sacrifice acceptable and pleasing to God. And my God will fully satisfy every need of yours according to his riches in glory in Christ Jesus. To our God and Father be glory forever and ever. Amen.

> *Greet every saint in Christ Jesus. The friends who are with me*
> *greet you. All the saints greet you, especially those of the*
> *emperor's household. The grace of the Lord Jesus Christ be with*
> *your spirit (Philippians 4:10-23).*

Paul now turns to one of the main reasons for writing to the Philippians: to express his gratitude for their help and generosity. Money matters can be a rather sensitive subject to speak or write about. While Paul wants them to know how thankful he is for their support, he must be careful not to suggest that he expected more from them than they had done so far. Also, he wants them to know he had learned not to complain about his physical and material circumstances, and that by God's power he could live both with need as well as with abundance.

The apostle expresses his appreciation for the concern of the Philippians, seen in sending a gift along with their messenger, Epaphroditus. Much as he enjoyed their material support, he rejoices even more at the thought that God will reward them richly for helping Paul in his need.

Although the passage before us seems to be of a more personal nature and of local interest, Paul's words of commendation for receiving financial aid, contain a number of important and fundamental principles that can guide us in the whole area of giving and receiving money in the work of the kingdom of God. If we listen carefully to the text we will find ourselves addressed by God's word at a number of points. We begin with Paul's words of appreciation for the Philippians' loving concern.

I. HIS APPRECIATION FOR THEIR CONCERN (v. 10)

"I rejoice in the Lord greatly that now at last you have revived your concern for me; indeed, you were concerned for me, but had no opportunity to show it." After calling on his readers to rejoice in the Lord (v. 4), he now confesses his feelings of joy at the thought of their loving care. The verb is in the past tense but in letters the past is often epistolary, i.e., seen from the standpoint of the readers of the letters, and so should be rendered as the present "I rejoice." The intensity of his feelings is underscored by the adverb "greatly" (*megalos*), which occurs only here in the New Testament. To rejoice "in the Lord" suggests the Lord is ultimately the source of Paul's joy. Also, it is in fellowship with the Lord that his joy thrives.

Paul has not yet mentioned their gift specifically but begins by expressing his appreciation for their loving concern. What takes us aback is the comment that "at last" their concern has flourished. At first blush this seems to be a slight criticism of their tardiness in sending him help. However, the following clause clarifies this: they had not had opportunity.

The verb for the "revival" of their concern for Paul is highly metaphorical. Literally the verb means to bloom afresh, like a bush or tree putting out new shoots or flowers in spring. Their thoughtful concern for Paul which had flourished once again was no doubt in Paul's mind when he thanked them for their "fellowship in the gospel" (1:5).

That Paul is not criticizing his readers for neglect is made clear in the explanatory statement: they lacked opportunity. Although their loving concern for Paul had been there all along they had no chance to express this concretely. Precisely what had kept them from supporting Paul financially in the more recent past is not stated. Were they too poor to send him help (cf. 2 Cor. 8:1,2)? Or was there no one available to make the long journey to Rome with the gift of the Philippians? Could it also be that Paul had discouraged them from sending him financial help for fear that the enemies of the church might charge him with pecuniary motives (cf. I Thess. 2:9)? Although Paul always appreciated material help when he received it, as far as we know he never asked for it. He did solicit moneys for others, of course. The gift from the Philippians had come unsolicited, and like a person rejoicing over the signs of spring after a hard winter, Paul rejoiced over the renewal of their concern for him.

The receipt of the gift from Philippi delivered by Epaphroditus, leads Paul not only to rejoice at the kindness of the church, but also to say something about his own approach to material things in general.

II. HIS ATTITUDE TOWARD THE NECESSITIES OF LIFE
(vv. 11-13)

A. The Attitude Expressed (vv. 11,12)

"Not that I am referring to being in need; for I have learned to be content with whatever I have. I know what it is to have little, and I know what it is to have plenty. In any and all circumstances I have learned the secret of being well-fed and of going hungry, of having plenty and of being in need."

Paul's gratitude for receiving material aid was not prompted by his difficult circumstances, by his need or by his lack of the necessities of life. He does not think of himself as one who is in dire financial straits and whose poverty has now been alleviated by the gift of the Philippians. He makes no statement on his needs, but wants his readers to know his words of thanks were not dictated by his wants. He then proceeds to give the reason.

"I have learned to be content in whatever circumstances I find myself." The verb "learned" does not suggest a specific time in Paul's life when he learned this lesson. It is what is called a "constative" aorist and embraces the entire life of the apostle; it sums up his learning experiences as a whole.

Paul uses an unusual word for "contentment" here (*autarkes*), found only here in this form in the New Testament (for another form of the noun, see 2 Cor. 9:8; 1 Tim. 6:6). Quite literally the word means "self-sufficient," and was used by Stoics as the essence of virtue. They thought of it as self-reliance because of inner resources. It described a person who was independent of people and things. Did Paul borrow this Stoic word? If he did, he transforms its meaning. He had to do this with much of the Greek vocabulary he employed. *Autarkes* expresses Paul's independence of outer circumstances, not because he felt self-sufficient but because he lived his life in dependence on God. "Our sufficiency is of God," he writes to the Corinthians (2 Cor. 3:5). "Be satisfied with what you have" (Heb. 13:5), seems to have been a general precept in the early church. Paul claims he is content in "whatever circumstances" he finds himself—"anywhere at any time" as the GNB has it.

He will now describe what it means to be content: "I know what it is to have little, and I know what it is to have plenty." Literally he confesses that he knows how to be brought low, to be humbled, perhaps even chastened. To have plenty quite literally means "to overflow," to have enough and to spare. Paul is not simply saying he has experienced both the extremes of poverty and of plenty, but he has learned to live with both extremes. "I know" is the equivalent of "I have learned" (v. 11). He has learned to live in the appropriate manner in poverty and in plenty. The usual opposite of being "humbled" is to be exalted. Here, however, the opposite of being brought low by economic need is to have more than enough to live on.

He has learned the secret of being well fed and of going hungry, of having more than enough and of having little. Paul has learned how to adapt to the vicissitudes of life. He employs a verb (*mueo*) which is found in the Greek mystery religions to describe the rites of initiation. Here, however, the verb is torn from that pagan background and describes Paul's initiation into the secrets of contentment. He can be full. The verb *chortazomai* was used for the fattening of animals but also of satisfying the physical needs of a hungry crowd (e.g., Mt. 14:20). The opposite is to go hungry—also something Paul experienced many times (I Cor. 4:11, "we go hungry"). He had learned to live with "too much" (I suppose too much would be more than the minimum) and "too little"—not enough to eat.

When one puts Paul's attitude toward the material things of life side by side with the promises of "sexual joy, narcotic paradise, communal contentment and dining ecstasy" that one hears from time to time in the Christian media, one feels ashamed. How far removed is the message of the apostle from the so-called "health and wealth doctrine" which promises believers material success, a bubbling personality and continuous health in this life.

In verse 13 Paul gives us the secret of his contentment. Lest any of the readers come to the conclusion that Paul is in a class all by himself, he will show his readers that the strength by which he is enabled to cope with the ever-changing circumstances of life is available to them also.

B. The Attitude Explained (v. 13)

"I can do all things through him who strengthens me." If one takes

Paul's claim quite literally, one might be led to think that nothing lay beyond the capabilities of the apostle. However, the context has to be taken into account. The "all things" must refer to the matters under consideration, namely the ability to be content in good and bad circumstances. If the verb "to be able" draws attention to Paul's ability to cope with the changing physical circumstances of life, the addition "by the one strengthening me" makes it clear that this ability to be content does not come from Paul's own inner resources. Paul is not boasting about Stoic self-sufficiency but rather points to the source of his strength, which is Christ.

Although the older English versions read "through Christ who strengthens me," the better Greek manuscripts do not have the word "Christ," although Christ is meant. The word "Christ" was inserted by later scribes, thinking perhaps that Paul would be misunderstood. This strengthening is an ongoing work of Christ in Paul's life, although Paul upon occasion uses the past tense as well (see I Tim. 1:12). We should remind ourselves of what the apostle says in 2 Corinthians 13:9,10 where he confesses that when he is weak, then he is truly strong. He can face both wealth and poverty, hunger and abundance, abasement and exaltation, not because he has steeled himself against the ups and downs of life but because Christ lives in him and he gives Paul the grace to be content.

III. HIS GRATITUDE FOR THEIR MATERIAL AID (vv. 14-20)

A. His Praise (vv. 14-16)

1. For Present Help (v. 14). "In any case, it was kind of you to share my distress." If the Philippians got the feeling (as some modern commentators have suggested) that Paul was saying "Thank you for your gift, but it wasn't necessary," Paul now removes such possible misunderstanding. He is in fact deeply grateful for their kindness. "Nevertheless, you did well." Just because Christ enables him to be content in all circumstances did not make their gift unnecessary, and he expresses his appreciation for their kindness. The word *kalos* means "well, beautifully," and with reference to outward appearance can signify "fitly" or "appropriately."

It was a beautiful thing to share with Paul in his distress. Their expression of kindness meant "to have fellowship in his distress." In 1:7 Paul called his readers "fellow-sharers" of God's grace. Also, he thanked God that they had shared with him in the gospel (1:5). And here he thanks them for sharing in his trials. He does not specify what kind of distress they shared with him, but the word *thlipsis* is wide enough to include both external sufferings as well as internal pressures, mental and spiritual difficulties. It is the word used frequently for the sufferings of the believers in the last days. In our passage it probably refers to the sufferings he had to endure as a prisoner. They have taken some of the burden of suffering from Paul's shoulders by sending him a financial gift.

2. For Past Kindness (vv. 15,16). "You Philippians indeed know that in the early days of the gospel, when I left Macedonia, no church shared with me in the matter of giving and receiving, except you alone. For even when I was in Thessalonica, you sent me help for my needs more than once."

While Paul acknowledges with gratitude the gift he received from his readers in the more recent past, he has not forgotten that they had participated in the ongoing work of the gospel "from the first day until now" (1:5). He did not really need to remind them of their past generosity, for he says, "You yourselves know." Only rarely does Paul in his letters address his readers by name as he does here: "You Philippians" (Gal. 3:1, "Galatians," and 2 Cor. 6:11, "Corinthians").

The Philippians had helped earlier "at the beginning of the gospel." What does he specifically mean by that ? Surely he is not saying he began to preach the gospel in Philippi, for he had spread the gospel for some fourteen years before he crossed over to Europe. Does he mean that although he had preached the gospel elsewhere for a long time, the mission to Macedonia was so important that he calls it the true "beginning" of his ministry. Perhaps he means his mission entered a new phase when he came to Macedonia; it was a decisive turning point in his missionary endeavors when he left the Asiatic mainland to begin the evangelization of Europe. It could be that Paul has the readers' perspective in mind when he speaks of the "beginning of the gospel." He would then mean "in the early days of your acquaintance with the gospel" (New International Version).

"After I departed from Macedonia" is in apposition to the "beginning of the gospel," and most likely refers to the time when Paul left Macedonia and settled in Corinth for a protracted ministry . Writing to the Corinthians later, Paul reminds them that he had robbed other churches so he might not be a burden to them, "for the brothers who came from Macedonia supplied what I needed" (2 Cor. 11:8,9). He is perhaps thinking of the coming of Silas and Timothy from Macedonia (Acts 18:5). They brought financial aid to Paul in Corinth and so it seems he did not have to spend all his time earning his daily bread but could give himself unreservedly to the proclamation of the good news. Macedonia basically means Philippi.

To put further emphasis on the generosity of the Philippians, he reminds them that "no church shared with me in the matter of giving and receiving, except you alone." To help others who are in financial need is called a "sharing" (*koinoneo*). Paul uses vocabulary from the world of business to describe the generosity of the Philippians: the nouns "giving" and "receiving" refer to monetary transactions. The NEB renders this vocabulary in more current terms: "my partners in payments and receipts." It may be, however, that the entire expression "sharing in giving and receiving" should be understood here as an idiomatic expression for friendship.

So generous had the Philippians been that even before Paul left Macedonia when he was still in Thessalonica, they sent help to meet his needs more than once. Quite literally the text says they sent help "not once but twice." This may be however, an idiomatic expression for "more than once." They began to contribute to the Pauline mission right from the beginning and they continued even after he left Macedonia. In his letters to the Thessalonians Paul does not mention he had received financial help from Philippi while he worked day and night not to be a burden to them (I Thess. 2:9). But perhaps it would have been embarrassing to the Thessalonians had he told them that others had supported him while he worked among them.

B. His Perspective (vv. 17,18)
"Not that I seek the gift, but I seek the profit that accumulates to your account. I have been paid in full and have more than enough; I am fully satisfied, now that I have received from Epaphroditus the gifts you sent, a fragrant offering, a sacrifice acceptable and pleasing to God."

Lest his readers should think that Paul, by expressing his gratitude for their gifts, betrays a hidden covetousness, he explains his heart is not set on their gifts but on what such generosity does for them. Although he is grateful for their support, he is even more grateful for the work of God's grace in their lives that led them to take such actions. Moreover, he rejoices at the thought that their generosity will accrue to their account.

Paul continues the language of commerce in verse 17. The word "fruit" is used here in the sense of advantage, profit or more likely with the meaning of "interest." By helping Paul they have made a deposit in the bank of heaven that will multiply at compound interest to their advantage. Although the verb "to increase"(*pleonazo*) is not ordinarily a business word, in this context it seems to take on commercial nuances, meaning "accruing" to their credit. Although generosity also brings returns in terms of spiritual benefits in this life, Paul is probably thinking of the life to come. Jesus also spoke of laying up treasures in heaven.

Another reason why he is not looking with greedy eyes for more financial help from his readers is because he has enough. Using commercial language once more (the word *apecho* is used for a receipt, something like "paid in full"), Paul writes: "Here, then, is my receipt for everything" (GNB). In fact, he has more than enough: "I am fully satisfied." The passive voice of the verb "to fill" (*pleroo*) suggests Paul was filled up by them; he did not fill himself.

This happened when Epaphroditus came to Paul from Philippi and brought him their donations (what Epaphroditus brought or how much is not stated). From commercial language Paul then switches to sacrificial language to describe their generosity: "a fragrant offering, an acceptable sacrifice, which is pleasing to God." In the Old Testament sacrifices that were acceptable to God were said to be a "sweet smell." By describing the gift of the Philippians as an offering with a lovely fragrance, Paul stresses its great worth. Such offerings bring pleasure to God. "Do not neglect to do good and to share what you have" writes the author of Hebrews, "for such sacrifices are pleasing to God" (13:16). Clearly then, giving of our financial resources to help others in need is part of our priestly service; it is an offering to God.

C. His Promise (v. 19)

"And my God will fully satisfy every need of yours according to his riches in glory in Christ Jesus." Paul is not suggesting that because his readers gave of their possessions to help him in his ministry, God was now obligated to supply all their material needs. However, he is confident God will help them in their physical needs. Since Christians often had to live in difficult financial circumstances, some commentators have suggested that "all your needs" has to do with their spiritual needs rather than the material. And if one puts this prayer beside the one in 1:9-11 where Paul prays for their spiritual needs, one cannot rule out the spiritual needs. The focus, however, seems to be on their earthly needs, including hardships, suffering, affliction and deprivation. If we read Paul's words as a wish-prayer and not as a guarantee that they will always have enough to eat, we are probably on the right track. Perhaps we should summarize Paul's thoughts in this way, "In return for your meeting my needs, I pray that my God may meet all your needs" (cf. Confraternity, Knox). Paul allows God the freedom to be God and to fulfil their earthly needs as he sees best (so Hawthorne).

Paul's wish-prayer for the Philippians is that God might supply all their needs, both spiritual and physical, "according to his riches in glory in Christ Jesus." God's resources are unlimited and Paul expresses the confidence that God will supply their needs lavishly as only he can, on a scale worthy of his wealth. Not only "from" his wealth, but in a manner that befits his wealth. No one can estimate the range and depth of God's richness (see Rom. 11:33).

But how are we to understand the prepositional phrase "in glory?" Does that mean that although they may lack many things here in life they will be richly rewarded when they get to glory? Or is the phrase to be connected with the verb "to supply," in the sense that God will supply all they need in a glorious manner? Perhaps it is best to connect it with the noun "riches," i.e., he will meet all the needs of the Philippians in keeping with his "glorious riches." As one who had walked with God for a long time and as a man who had learned to be content even in dire circumstances, Paul confidently prays that God might abundantly supply the needs of his readers. What is lacking here on earth will, to be sure, be fulfilled "in glory." The sufferings of the present are not worthy to be compared with the glory that shall be revealed. And all this will happen because they are in fellowship with Christ Jesus through whom God has promised to meet them in their needs.

D. His Paean (v. 20)

"To our God and Father be glory forever and ever. Amen." This doxology is a fitting conclusion to Paul's words of appreciation for the gifts of the Philippians, but it also brings the letter to an appropriate end. Doxologies are found rather frequently in the writings of Paul and they have more or less the same structure. First, the person to whom the praise is ascribed is mentioned: "To God our Father." Since the Greek has only one article for both nouns here, we could translate "To our God and Father." In verse 19 Paul used the intensely personal "my God" but here he unites with his readers in ascribing this paean of praise to God.

As in other doxologies, Paul ascribes *doxa* (glory) to God. To ascribe glory to God does not mean Paul is adding something he does not already have; he is simply acknowledging the fact that all glory belongs to God. A third item in the doxology is the temporal expression "forever and ever." Eternity is viewed as a succession of ages, and Paul's ascription of glory is not limited to this age only but also to the ages to come, forever and ever.

Christians carried over the Jewish practice of endorsing prayers, doxologies, curses and blessings, with the Hebraic "Amen," "so let it be." The writer probably expected the readers to join him in this Amen, as the letter was read in the church.

IV CONCLUSION (vv. 21-23)

A. Greetings (vv. 21, 22)

"Greet every saint in Christ Jesus. The friends who are with me greet you. All the saints greet you, especially those of the emperor's household." Although Paul generally follows the letter style of his day, he does not use the standard expressions such as "farewell," or "good luck." Instead he sends personal greetings filled with Christian content. Since Paul no doubt dictated his letters, it may be that at this point he took the pen from the hand of his amanuensis and wrote the closing greetings with his own hand (see Gal. 6:11). And in order to avoid any suggestion that he was partial to one or the other member in the Philippian church, he mentions no names but simply greets "every saint in Christ Jesus." Implied is that the church leaders (mentioned in 1:1) would make sure this letter be read in the hearing of the entire church. One might have expected Paul to mention the Philippian jailor or Lydia, his first converts, but no, he wants all members of the church to receive his greetings.

Paul also sends greetings from "the friends who are with me." In the next verse "all the saints" send greetings, and so these friends must refer to a smaller group of co-workers, such as Timothy (2:19) and Luke (Acts 27:1). How large this circle of friends was we do not know. Who all the saints were is also not clear, but the word may include the entire Christian community of Rome, even though that would make the expression "with me" a bit artificial.

Special mention is made of the saints that belong to the emperor's household. This would not necessarily refer to the emperor's family or relations but to the great number of slaves and freedmen from whose ranks the imperial service was staffed. These were found throughout the empire in the provinces but there was a concentration of them in Rome. Among these Romans were believers.

It may even be that these Christians in the imperial service had had special contacts with Philippi in their official capacity. Here we have clear evidence of the gospel beginning to penetrate government circles.

B. Benediction (v. 23)

"The grace of the Lord Jesus Christ be with your spirit." Paul began his letter with grace and he concludes it with the same rich word. The fountainhead of this grace is the Lord Jesus Christ. He is the one who bestows his grace freely upon undeserving humankind, and he will also sustain the Philippian church by his grace. Although Paul frequently wishes that God's grace might be with his readers, here we have the rather unusual expression "with your spirit." Christ's grace is to rest and abide upon each member of the congregation. "Spirit" is used here very much like "person"; "with your spirit" is not different in meaning from "with you."

We are not quite sure whether the Amen, found in a good many manuscripts, is genuine or whether it is a natural addition by a copyist. If genuine, then it may reflect Paul's own response to the prayer of verse 23, or it may suggest the response of the congregation when the letter is read in the church.

Review Questions

1. *Could a hearty thanks for the receipt of a material gift be misunderstood?*

2. *What is the difference between contentment and self-sufficiency?*

3. *Which of the two is easier for the believer to handle: to have too little or to have too much?*

4. *How had the generosity of the Philippians expressed itself in the past?*

5. *Their financial help was appreciated by Paul. Was it also of benefit to the Philippians?*

6. *What assurance have we in the New Testament that God will supply all our material needs? Do Christians also die of hunger?*

Selected English Language Commentaries On Philippians

Barclay, William. *The Letters to the Philippians. Colossians and Thessalonians.* The Daily Bible Study Series. Philadelphia: Westminster Press, 1959.

Bruce, F.F. *Philippians.* A Good News Commentary. San Francisco: Harper and Row, 1983.

Hawthorne, Gerald F. *Philippians.* Word Biblical Commentary, 43. Waco: Word Books, 1983 .

Loh, I-Jin and Nida, Eugene. *A Translator's Handbook on Paul's Letter to the Philippians.* Stuttgart: United Bible Societies, 1977.

Martin, Ralph P. *The Epistle of Paul to the Philippians.* The Tyndale New Testament Commentaries. Grand Rapids: Wm. B. Eerdmans, 1959.

Mueller, J.J. *The Epistles of Paul to the Philippians and Philemon.* The New International Commentary on the New Testament. Grand Rapids: Wm. B. Eerdmans, 1955.

O'Brien, Peter T. *The Epistle to the Philippians.* Commentary on the Greek Text. Grand Rapids: Wm. B. Eerdmans, 1991.

Pickford, John H. *Paul's Spiritual Autobiography.* Toronto: Evangelical Publishers, 1949.

Other Books in the Luminaire Series

- *The Church in Pagan Society*
  Studies in I Corinthians
  David Ewert

- *The Church Under Fire*
  Studies in Revelation
  David Ewert

- *The Power of God in a Broken World*
  Studies in Ephesians
  Erwin Penner

- *When the Church Was Young*
  Studies in I & II Thessalonians
  David Ewert

All books available from your local bookstore or from:

Kindred Productions
169 Riverton Ave., Winnipeg, Manitoba R2L 2E5
315 S. Lincoln, Hillsboro, Kansas 67063